The Other Woman

Judy Mamou
with Ingrid Reininga-Scott

VISION HOUSE PUBLISHERS
Santa Ana, California 92705

The Other Woman

Copyright © 1977 by Vision House Publishers, Santa Ana, California 92705.

Library of Congress Catalog Card Number 77-92170
ISBN Number 0-88449-028-9

Printed in the United States of America.

TO

My husband Jimmy whom I love very much. Your faith in God was the instrument that led me to Christ. Thank you for loving God and thank you for loving me.

CONTENTS
TABLE OF CONTENTS

PREFACE

I wanted to die.

I sat in my Waikiki penthouse, the world at my feet, and wondered how to end it.

"Like an X-rated movie," I thought. "That's how I've lived. That's how I should die."

I pictured them finding my body—diamond rings on each finger, mink coat draped over my legs. Chest bare, perhaps.

"Why did she do it?" they'd ask. "She had everything. Wealth, beauty, fame. A good husband. The companionship of movie stars and professional athletes. And she was so young, too."

But I had never been young. I had been fifty at the age of five, so what did that make me at thirty?

I looked around the room. The diamond rings that weren't on my fingers sat side by side in my jewelry box, waiting to be worn. Three minks hung in the closet; the others were still back in San Francisco. The rest of the room looked like I'd raided a department store—pantsuits, halter tops, bikinis, evening gowns, negligees, eyelashes, wigs—all strewn around like yesterday's hand-me-downs.

And there were the less obvious assets: the bank accounts, the income property, the stocks and bonds, the Cadillacs. The men, the glamour, the attention, the celebrity status I had worked so hard for. And the freedom—the fact that no man was my master; no one told me what to do.

Then I looked in the mirror. That, too, was deceptive. A full-bodied figure, dark hair, pale, smooth, unwrinkled skin. A facade. A distorted image of what was inside.

"There is nothing behind this skin and these bones," I thought. "There is no one there."

My years as a prostitute and a stripper had finally caught up with me. I had sinned until I could sin no more, and now I was utterly empty. My soul? I felt I had no soul. I could only feel a void, so I filled it up the only way that was left—with Seconal, scotch, Valium, Darvon and speed. This was no dramatic ploy designed to scare someone—I wanted out, and I meant business.

As I closed my eyes, waiting to die, I saw the leers and stares of thousands of men, flashing their motel keys and money at me as I danced by, grabbing at me, telling me how beautiful I was. I saw myself lying to them, stealing from them, cursing at them under my breath. I saw myself sneaking out on my husband, then throwing fits of jealous rage when he was a minute late coming home. I saw the drunken stupors, the hangovers, the dope parties.

And at my funeral, I saw my two sons, faces turned away.

It had been hell. I was glad I was getting out.

1
Abused!

One thing I know for sure: prostitutes are made, not born. My own life of prostitution actually began when I was five. Before then, my life was like a fairy tale in reverse, with the happily-ever-after part coming first. Then I had everything. The loving mother. The doting father. The little white farmhouse in Oklahoma.

My first five years on that farm were like a favorite old blanket—warm, secure, dependable. I would awaken to the sound of farm news on the radio, the smell of hot coffee and bacon in the air. In the kitchen, Mom would smile at me from the stove and say, "How would you like your eggs this morning, honey?" Dad would wink and ask, "Did my little girl sleep well last night?"

After breakfast I would snuggle deep into Mom's lap while she twisted my hair into Shirley Temple curls. Then I'd run out to play in the hayloft, by the chicken coop or behind the barn. Every once in a while I'd go back into the house, and Mom would be there, smelling of cinnamon or cloves or freshly baked bread. At night, after dinner, I'd fall asleep in front of the fireplace, lulled by the sound of crickets.

But all that disappeared in the space of one day—just disappeared. I was playing out front in my sundress when it happened. A rickety old car drove up, swirling dust in my eyes. A kind of pretty lady got out and walked toward me. She looked at me hard, like she couldn't believe I was real—like I was strange and familiar all at the same time.

"So this is Judy," she said. "Yes, ma'am." I looked down. Her feet were crushing a cigarette into the lawn.

She went inside the house, and for a moment I felt like running.

"That lady isn't happy," I remember thinking. But she was already coming out again, and then all of a sudden everything happened at once. Her arms were around me, but it wasn't a real hug like Mom's, and Mom was making funny sobbing sounds like my dog did when she was hurt. Dad was crying, too. I'd never seen him cry before.

"Judy, you're my girl," the lady was saying. "You're going to live with me from now on. You don't belong here, so say goodbye."

At first I was numb, like a fish packed in ice, and I looked at Mom, but she was sort of stooping and rocking back and forth and moaning. Dad was saying, "No." "No." "No." Each "no" a little sentence. And he was hitting the side of the wooden house with his hand. I just stood there with my mouth open.

"Mommy?" They wouldn't let anyone take me away. They'd never even left me with a babysitter. Then the lady started pulling at me, dragging me away with her bony fingers. I grabbed Mom's apron.

"Mommy, Mommy, take me." Mom was pulling me one way, and the lady another. Then Mom did a strange thing. She let go.

All of a sudden, I was in the battered old car. She was in there with me, and Mom and Dad were on the outside. I was screaming and kicking my feet.

"Mommy. Mommy. Get me out of here. I'll be good, I promise, Mommy." I had my face plastered against the window; tears were running down my cheeks and smearing into the glass. The car was filled with ugly cigarette smoke, but I could still see: Mom and Dad were getting smaller and smaller.

"From now on, call me Mommy," the lady said as they disappeared over the horizon.

I sat curled into a ball in the back seat, my hands over my eyes. "If I can't see this lady, she won't be here," I thought. I cried so hard on that trip that I thought my head would explode. I don't know how long we drove or what we passed, but I do remember what greeted me when we got there—a tiny little apartment and a girl named Donna, who came out to stare at me.

"She's your new sister," the lady said, "so I hope you kids get along and don't give me no trouble." She walked into the

Judy and her older sister, Donna.

house. Donna waited until she was gone and then stuck out her tongue at me. There would be no help from that quarter.

I remember standing by that old, beat-up car, literally not knowing what to do.

"I have to stay outside so Mommy will see me when she comes," I thought, but the sun was so bright on my swollen eyes I could hardly see. The heat pounded into my head. Still, I stayed there for what seemed like hours. Finally, I went into the house and sat by myself near the living room window. I watched the bright white sky outside slowly take on golden tones, then softer pink ones, and finally mellow out to a dull gray. At last all turned black. Still, I waited. It never once occurred to me that no one was coming.

"They must've gotten lost," I thought later, lying ramrod-straight in the bed they had given me in Donna's room. She lay across the room, watching me. "This is your real home, you know. You're here to stay," she said.

"She's trying to get me to cry," I thought. "I'll never cry in front of her."

For a while she was quiet. Then, "This is your real Mom, and not those farm people. Mom hated you when you were born and gave you to them to raise, but now she decided to get you back."

She paused. "You'll never see those farm people again." I turned my head to the wall. The tears were flooding down, and the effort of not crying aloud was choking and burning my throat. At last she gave up and fell asleep. Finally, I could let go. Tears of terror, of loneliness, of abandonment flooded me, washed over me. Why had my mother let go of my hand? I couldn't get that moment out of my head. It hurt so much, and I just couldn't comprehend it. And why hadn't they come to get me yet. My body was weak from strain, and I felt that if Mom and Dad didn't come right that minute, I would throw up, or die, or something.

"They'll come tomorrow for sure. When I wake up, they'll be here," I kept telling myself.

At first when I woke up, I didn't remember where I was. I stumbled out to the strange kitchen. Donna saw me and snuggled closer to her mother.

"Well, it's about time," my new mother said. "Here, eat 'em." She plopped a plate of cold eggs in front of me, the yellow and white run together and hard. She saw me looking at them.

"Listen, sister, you'll eat those eggs or you'll wear them. You've had a free ride for five years, and now the party's over." Then I saw it: she had a switch in her hand. I didn't know for sure what it was for, but I knew the look on her face. I gagged on the first bite of eggs and began the next one.

"You'll have to do better than that," she said, but she put the switch down.

After breakfast I sat by the window again. Soon Donna came in.

"You might as well give up looking. They're not coming," she said. "You can cry till you turn blue, but they won't come. You're ours, now."

I turned away from her.

"Don't act so stuck up, smarty pants. Mom can beat that out of you," she said.

"My real Mommy will come to get me, you'll see."

All afternoon I waited. Where were they? I must've slept after a while, because I jumped when a car door slammed.

"Your Daddy's here," my new mother said. "Don't get all steamed up. I mean your new Daddy."

Suddenly a man was in the house, kissing her.

"Well, well, what have we got here?" he said when he saw me. I crouched into the corner of the sofa.

"This is Judy, honey, remember? Remember I told you I was going to keep her from now on? Say hello to your new Daddy, Judy."

"Hey, what's wrong? Cat got your tongue?" He picked me up and gave me a big hug.

"Hey, don't cry, honey. What are all those tears for? I love little girls. In fact, you can be my own little princess if you want to. How would you like that?"

A week went by. It seemed I had been away from the farm forever. My new mother was hitting me a lot, especially when Dad left for work. I would catch it if I got dirty, catch it if I forgot my sweater, catch it for just looking at her the wrong way. I didn't know what the wrong way was; I just knew she thought I was spoiled and was out to get me for it. I found the best way to stay out of trouble was to act quiet. Don't laugh. Don't smile. Don't talk. Don't think. Don't care. Just stay out of her way.

After ten days or so, I stopped sitting at the window and sat in my room most of the time. I dreamed about the farm every minute: it was an enchanted land for me now, a land of sunshine and spring flowers. Mom was the kindly queen, and Dad was the king who would someday come to fetch me.

Meanwhile, my new Dad was a help, at least at first. He was a house painter by trade, and when he couldn't get work, he would go to the neighboring towns to gamble. When he was gone, Mother would be unhappy and beat me a lot, but when he came back, he made everyone laugh. Best of all, when he was home, the beatings stopped. I began to love him because I thought he could save me from her.

One night, Mother took Donna shopping. I remember how happy I was. That meant Dad and I would be alone.

"Come sit on my lap, sweetie," he said after they left. "Let your Daddy love you a little."

"Why are you always gloomy, Princess? Don't you like your new home?"

I started to cry, and he wiped my tears with a big blue handkerchief.

"Let me tell you something, honey. I know this is all confusing to you, but you do belong here. Your mommy couldn't take care of you when you were born, so she gave you to MaRue and Ardean, those people on the farm. Just for a while 'til she could get on her feet. And now you're back with us again, so we can be one big happy family."

"When will Mommy and Daddy come to get me?" I asked.

I buried my head in his shoulder and cried. He kissed me on the cheek and neck, and I cried even harder.

"I mean my real Mommy and Daddy," I sobbed.

He let me cry for a long time, and finally I fell asleep on his chest.

"Come on, honey, let me tuck you in," he said later, and he carried me to the bedroom. He started to undress me, and, looking back, I think perhaps everything might've been okay that night if he hadn't seen the black and blue marks on my bare behind. But he did.

"What's this?" he said. He held me up to the mirror in his room, and I saw it, too. My tiny rear end was so puffy and swollen it was completely distorted.

"Oh, baby," he moaned. I remember well the sound of that moan, because it was so strange—a mixture of pain, grief, shock and one other element. Excitement.

What followed is, after thirty-odd years, still too painful to tell except in the most impersonal tones. He grabbed me up in his arms and kissed me over and over again, on all parts of my body.

"What's he doing?" I thought. My heart was like a sledge

hammer, beating my chest from the inside, and my stomach turned over in revulsion. I didn't know what he was doing, or why, but instinctively I knew it was wrong.

My first impulse was to fight, but then another instinct took over: to survive. Just lie perfectly still, clench your teeth, and squeeze your eyes shut. Hear nothing, see nothing, feel nothing. The only person left in this world for you to trust has just turned on you in the most painful and degrading way.

Finally, after a long, long time, he seemed to be sleeping. I lay there, staring at the ceiling. I was only five, but even then, I knew: I would never be the same. The beatings from Mother had only hurt me on the outside, but this—this had scarred my soul.

"Good-night, Princess," he said as he tucked me in.

"How can he call me 'Princess' when I'm not pretty anymore?" I thought.

Judy of Sunnybrook Farm had already begun to die, and from the ashes, Tara, the prostitute, was beginning to emerge.

2 The Other Girl

I'd like to be able to say that after a few months of living in that house I got used to it, that after a while it seemed I had always lived there, but that's just not true. In the ten years I spent there only one thing really changed: me.

Without admitting it to myself, without even knowing it, I was starting to lose that little girl from the farm, to surround her with, and finally bury her under, a giant shield of steel. It was a cold and loveless house I was in, and I gradually decided that the only way to live through it was to put my own emotions on ice.

But every night, when they all were asleep, those tears I'd held back all day would come flooding out, and I would cry for long, long hours. In the first years there, I never got enough sleep, and I was constantly red-eyed and sick to my stomach. I didn't tell anyone—there was no one to tell, no one to comfort me. It seemed like I was completely alone.

Mother was almost proud of the way she was "disciplining" me.

"Judy, come here," she'd call whenever her friends were over. "Come here and show Dolores what you got for being bad today." Then I'd have to go in the living room and pull down my pants for her friends to see. They always seemed surprised at all the welts and bruises.

"See what I got to go through?" Mother would say.

Report card time was the worst. On those days she would wait outside for me with a switch in her hand.

"Did you get another 'C' in conduct?" she'd yell when I was still half a block away. To her, an average "C" meant I was bad, and she was ready to whip me for it. If my grades were okay, she found other excuses to beat me.

Looking back on it now, over thirty years later, I can see what I couldn't see then. Mother, like every other mother who is concerned about her children, was doing what she thought was right. If a child "misbehaved," she thought you slapped now and asked questions later. Part of my problem was that for the first five years of my life I had been raised so differently, and the adjustment to a new way of discipline wasn't easy to come by. Also, her definition of "misbehaving" was much broader than Mom MaRue's, to say the least.

I think now that Mother must've been quite unhappy when I was young. Dad wasn't around, we had very little money, and we lived in somewhat squalid conditions. It must've been all too easy to take it out on a child she probably felt guilty about anyway.

But at that time, of course, I couldn't see any of this. All I could see or feel then was that I was being mistreated.

In those days I didn't talk much around the house, or smile, either. I didn't see any reason to. I just kept a neutral look pasted on my face and tried to get through each day, one day at a time.

"Honey, sometimes I think your Mommy keeps all the trees around here stripped bare, getting sticks for your beatings," said a neighbor one day. "I don't know how you take it."

I took it because there was no way out. "Just exist," I told myself. "Just exist. Someday you'll get out of here, and then you'll be the boss."

Meanwhile, I had to survive, so in self-defense I became almost two people. There was the Judy I presented to the world, who was quiet, seemingly respectful, careful to try to do right, but completely a robot. She seemed to have no feelings, no warmth, no child-like love or affection, but then, she told herself, she had no pain, either. No one could touch her. Nothing could hurt her. Hit her and she didn't cry. Caress her and she didn't respond. She was invisible, really, of no consequence or importance to anyone but herself. A frail bag of bones whose heartbeat, if someone had cared to measure it, would have been negligible.

The other Judy, the "real" me, was a small, hurting little creature, a Bambi who had lost her mother. She felt the pain of those beatings, she suffered when she was abused, and she lived every moment in fear and dread. She was the one who felt dirty and ashamed and didn't know why. She was the one who knew something was always terribly wrong, but didn't quite know what. At night, when everyone was asleep and she could allow herself to soften and be herself again, she was seven or eight or nine; during the day, she felt like ninety-nine.

These were the two identities that began to be formed in me, without my even knowing it. In those tender years, they were completely intertwined and overlapping, but as the years passed, they were to become more and more distinct, arming themselves to do fierce battle for my soul.

In fact, that battle had already begun. It took place mostly at night in the form of a horrible recurring nightmare. In this dream, Mother was dead, and I saw myself, as a seven-year old, being led up to her casket.

"Kiss your mother good-bye," someone would say, and I would lean over her body, eyes closed, to do that. But always in the dream my eyes would open, and always I would do the same thing—spit in her face, and then walk away, smug, smiling. These nightmares gave me great pleasure until I woke up from them. Then the tears would start, the guilt and the shame.

"How can you do that?" I'd ask myself. "She is your mother. How can you be so bad?" Had I known how to pray, I probably would have been down on my knees in those mornings, begging for forgiveness, that's how guilty I felt. The only thing that kept me from going mad then was the memory of how I had been treated on the farm. Somehow, my little girl's mind understood, even then, that, for the most part, it was my parents who were wrong, not I. I had been loved on the farm, I had been given self-respect and treated like a human being. Had God not allowed me those first five years, I'm sure the following ten would've destroyed me.

There was one other thing that saved me in those years, and which, in very real ways, kept me alive. It was my new Grandma, my mother's mother, and she did one very simple, but essential, thing for me. She loved me. I would count the days until her visits. She came on the bus, and I would sit on the bench by the hour, waiting to see her face.

"Grandma!" I shouted when she got off, and I'd jump into her arms and nearly knock her over. Then we'd both kiss and cry.

"How's my little darlin'?" she'd say, and I'd bury my head in her soft chest.

"Oh, Grandma, Grandma. Thanks for coming," I'd whisper.

I remember a little game we used to play called, "It shall come to pass." She told me to make a wish and then open my Bible to any spot.

"Just open it, sweetheart," she'd say. "There's all sorts of good promises in it, so make a wish to God." When I opened it, if I found the words "It shall come to pass" on that page, she said it meant God would give me my wish. One day I saw the words, "Deliver us from evil" on one of those pages. Tears came into my eyes before I could stop them.

"Why, what's wrong, honey?" Grandma said, fumbling for her lace hanky.

"Nothing," I said, but I was lying. It had hit me just

then, seeing those words, that it was only a game we were playing. There was no one I knew in those days who could deliver me from the evil of that house.

Gram's visits would always go fast, and pretty soon I'd be walking her back to the bus again.

"Please let her bus be late," I'd pray. "Don't let her leave me here alone." But her bus always came, on time, and she always stooped down to give me a kiss.

"You be good for your Mommy, now, you hear?" she'd say, and the big bus doors would slam shut behind her. Then I'd have to walk back to the house alone to face the three of them.

Things were terrible with Dad in those grammar school years. He had what he called "our business arrangement."

"You scratch my back, and I'll scratch yours," he said, but I always knew he was talking about more than scratching backs. The worst thing about it was that he was so nice to me when other people were around. He'd kid me and play games with me and bring me toys—anything to get me loving him. Just like a normal Dad. Then, when it seemed I was trusting him most, he would change.

"Judy, come here," he'd call from his room whenever we were alone. My heart would sink.

"I can't do it," I'd tell myself. My stomach would revolt just remembering what went on in there. Never once in all those years did he force me to have complete intercourse with him, and he always tried to be gentle with me. Still, at age nine, I knew more about sex than most girls did at nineteen. I knew it changed people, made them into selfish monsters who would do anything, no matter how sickening, to make themselves feel good. When I was in that room with him, my Dad was no longer my Dad but some stranger who made me feel ugly and ashamed.

The worst times came when Mother and Donna would leave the house after I'd already gone to bed. I'd be sound asleep, and all of a sudden, there he'd be, pushing away the dolls in my tiny bed.

"Oh, no!" I'd whimper, still half asleep.

"You better be nice to me, or I'll make sure your Momma gets you," he'd say. And then, in a nicer voice, "Oh, honey, you're so sweet." I'd stare straight at the ceiling as he fondled and caressed me, not even knowing why he did all those things. It was all so strange to me, so urgent and tense, and I think now my young mind was literally in a state of shock for years about all that.

After Dad left, I would feel so lonely. In those years, as sick as our relationship was, he was still the only friend I had. He was my savior, I thought, and yet he was my torturer as well. That man tore me apart.

Sometimes, when I had nightmares about Mother, he would be in them, too, and I'd wake screaming, wet with fear; if I killed both of them off in my dreams, who would be left? I would scream and scream, into the darkness, but no one ever came in to ask why.

The next morning I was always sure Mother knew, the way she would pick on me, curse at me. At times I thought she was playing games with me, that she knew and she was just waiting to catch Dad and me. That, my child-mind knew, would be the end. The whole family would explode, break apart, all because of me.

I remember one of the worst times, a time fraught with so much hope at first and so much despair at the end. Dad had taken me on a hunting trip with his friends, and I felt so good, getting away from the house. It was a special day, and, as it wore on, I was almost happy. The woods were orange and golden, and Dad looked to me like the most handsome man there, always ready with a joke or a story. We all loved him. At night we sang around the fire, and Dad brought me lots of hot cider to drink.

I was almost asleep when he came to my sleeping bag. "Oh, no! Oh, Daddy, go away. Everybody'll see us." I was frantic. I had never dreamed he'd do anything with all those people around.

"Shh! Just shut up and let me worry about that."

He climbed in the oversized bag with me and began

touching me, whispering to me about all the things he had done with other women and girls.

"Stop. Stop. Oh, please be quiet." Already I was crying, I was so nervous. I knew they'd find us, and I was sure everyone would blame me.

"You just mind your Daddy, and do what I say," he said, this time in a louder voice.

"Oh, Daddy, I think I'm going to be sick." And I was. I threw up all over that sleeping bag.

Everyone woke up. "Take her home, Joe," they said. "Isn't that what you want, honey?"

"Yes, please Daddy. I want my Mommy," I said, and at that point, I did.

"We'll talk about it in the morning," he said, and he moved over to his own sleeping bag. He was really mad. All night I lay awake, wondering if I'd live through the next day. I had never seen him so angry. We drove in silence most of the way home, my stomach jumping over itself on the bumpy road. Right before we got there, he said, "You know I'll have to tell your Mother about this. You spoiled my trip, and I waited so long."

By the time we pulled up to the house, I was praying to be dead. I knew he would make up some story about why he was mad at me, and then I'd really get it. He walked into the house. I ran to the backyard and hid behind a tree. I saw Mother coming, and I pounded the tree with my hand, over and over. I had promised myself I'd never cry again, but I had to, just this once more.

She had her belt out and she was coming at me.

"You little brat. You'll be sorry you ever lived. Aren't you grateful for anything?"

I stopped crying. I could still cry over him, but not her. I remember how the belt felt as it slapped against my cold legs. The welts were forming on top of older welts. Dad was in the window, watching. Towards the end, he came out, but he never lifted a finger in my defense. When she was finally through, they went in the house together, his arm around her.

"And after you went to so much trouble to take her. Take Donna next time," she said.

I hurt too much to sit, so I stood there behind the tree until it got dark, just stood there alone. That night I stole an envelope and a stamp from Mother's drawer and wrote my first letter.

"Dear Mom and Dad,

"Could you please come and take me to the farm now? I'm not spoiled anymore, and I'll be good if you come. I miss you so much.

Your loving daughter,

Judy."

3 Sweet Sixteen

It was in high school, I think, that I finally began to crawl out from under the misery, to take charge of my own life. The transformation began slowly, and for a while those two differing sides of my personality hung in perfect balance.

I was the "soft" Judy at school, the one who needed attention and friendships like other people need food and air to breathe. I figured the way to get it was to be the best in everything.

"Hey, Judy. Saw you score twenty-two points yesterday. How'd you get so good at basketball?" a guy would yell.

"When you got it, you got it," I'd yell back, and my heart would beat wildly.

"He noticed me! He thinks I'm just as good as anybody else!"

Although I excelled in basketball, track, softball, school plays and majorettes, Mother and Dad never came to see me in any of these activities, and that hurt me almost more than anything they ever did to me. It also made the activities them-

selves more important. They weren't just games to me, they were hard work. My whole sense of identity, so stifled and repressed at home, had to blossom at school or it would wither and die. I was nobody at home; I had to be somebody at school.

The big blessing in those years came in the form of two friends, Colleen and another girl named Judy. "The Three Musketeers"—that's what everybody called us because they knew we would do anything for each other. We were inseparable as we consumed large pepperoni pizzas, made prank phone calls and stayed up all night giggling.

"Let's all break our dates tonight and watch the late, late show."

"Think the guys'll be mad?"

"We can tell 'em we talked about them all night."

So that's what we'd do.

Or we'd walk on the beach (my family had moved to California by then), go hiking, or spend long hours on the phone, sharing our secrets. But as close as I was to them, never once did I tell them about the thing with Dad. I guess I didn't want to think about it myself when I was away from it, so I was always pushing it out of my mind. It made me feel too different at a time when I was craving acceptance.

I don't know which meant more to me in those days, being out someplace with Judy and Colleen or hanging around Judy's house. I loved that house. Judy was the oldest of six kids, and it fell to her to bandage toes and kiss scraped knees. The house was always full of noise, teasing, laughter and love. Most amazing to me was the fact that never once in all those years at Judy's did I hear anyone get angry at anyone else.

But I would always have to go home again, and that experience was like walking from a warm, colorful, spring garden into the middle of an empty deep freeze. Mother seemed more unhappy than ever. You could see it in the slouch of her shoulders, hear it in the edge to her voice.

"And where you been today, getting into more trouble?"

"Trying out for cheerleader."

"What makes you think they'd pick you?"

"They didn't."

"Well, good. Now you'll have more time to get something done around here. This place is a mess."

Or she'd come after me, cigarette in hand.

"If I ever catch you smoking, I'll give you such a beating you'll wish you'd never been born." So. in rebellion, Judy, Colleen and I would go behind the house and chain smoke until we were sick. At times like those, the more hardened side of me seemed to take over, the side filled with bitterness and hatred.

My rebellion, though, was mostly mental. Instead of quietly "taking it," the way I had when I was younger, I began to curse my mother in my mind, using the same words for her that she always used for me. After a while I got used to thinking them, but it took longer to accept myself as the kind of person who was so hateful. I'd curse her in my mind and then say, "What am I doing?" Sometimes I literally didn't know who I was. The tension was making me a nervous wreck.

In those years, all I really wanted was for Mom and Dad to leave me alone, but unfortunately, neither of them could, especially Dad. It was obvious that I wasn't the skinny little five-year-old he had started molesting so long ago, and the more I grew up, the more he sought me out.

"You're looking real nice, honey," he used to say. "You ain't gonna forget your old Daddy, are you? You ain't gonna forget who's boss around here?"

What was even worse was that most of the privileges all my friends earned through doing chores, I earned through doing favors for Dad. I know that's awful, but he knew I needed to escape from the house, so he'd wait until a dance or a big basketball game was coming up and say, "If you put me in a good mood, I'll see to it your mother lets you go."

I'd toss and turn and lose sleep for two or three evenings, determined to turn him down. Then I'd go to school and hear everyone talking about the big game. I'd come home, look at him, and say, "I just can't." But in the end, I usually ended up giving him what he wanted, always stopping just short of complete intercourse. Afterwards, at the game or the dance, I had to try extra hard to blot out the memories enough to even enjoy myself.

In those days, I blamed him completely for what he "made" me do, but today I see the painful truth: I did have a choice, and I chose wrongly. I was selling myself, body and soul, for a trip to the movies or a Friday night basketball game. I was buying the semblance of a normal childhood, bits and pieces of happiness wherever I could find them.

This, I know now, was the beginning of my prostitution, and I cringe in shame when I think of it. And all the while I promised myself, "Someday I'll be in control." Because I had never had a personal relationship with a God Who could befriend me in such situations, those words were the only bedtime prayer I knew for years.

So I led my double life—outwardly happy and carefree at school, battered and abused at home. One day in particular seemed, even then, to symbolize how different those two lives were. Colleen and I had been invited to Christmas dinner at Judy's. As I looked around the table, I couldn't imagine what it would be like to live here all the time. But the longer the day wore on, the more I felt like I belonged. Didn't everyone call me "honey?" Hadn't Judy s Mom said she felt like I was one of her own?

On the way home that night, I told myself that nothing would make me lose that glow. I would carry the day's warm memories to bed with me, wrap them around me like a blanket and snuggle down to sleep with them.

I was still in a dreamy mood as I walked in. The tree had a bit of token tinsel on it, a few unwrapped presents were stuffed underneath, and almost all the bulbs were burned out. It took me a minute to see that Dad was sitting on the couch with only his robe on.

"Your Mother just left to do some last minute shopping, honey, so I thought it would be a good time to exchange gifts," he said. "What do you have for me?"

My insides turned to water, and I felt a dampness under my arms. Not tonight! Why did he have to ruin this day, too? How stupid I'd been to think I could escape, could feel normal for once.

I stood there, numb, and felt the despair of all the years engulf me. *This* was my family, not that other one I'd spent the day with. This was my life, and I had to live it. There was no one who loved me, I thought, and no way out.

I still don't know how I got through that evening except by gritting my teeth, forcing a smile and concentrating on places far away. All the while I kept repeating, "He's sick. He's sick, and I hate him." For years after that, Christmas always depressed me.

Gradually I found the best way to survive was to live by some narrow guidelines. The first rule of my private code was "hands off." If a boy tried to do more than kiss me, I thought he was insulting me, telling me I was cheap. I didn't need that; I had enough of it at home.

So whenever I did date, it was on a purely friendship basis. The only boy I ever really liked was Mike, a gawky teenager with brown eyes and slightly buck teeth.

"What rock did you find him under?" Mother would say. All I could see, though, was his winning smile, his warm sense of humor, and the fact that he never tried anything with me. My love for him was perhaps the only innocent, unconditional, child-like love I've ever felt for anyone; my dreams of him helped me wait out the hours until school started again each morning.

Mother, of course, knew she had another weapon to use against me, and one night, as I was getting dressed for a school dance, she announced flatly, for no reason, that she wouldn't drive me.

"Sorry," she said with a slight smile.

I refused to cry. With great casualness, I waited one whole hour. Then I walked out the door, being careful not to slam it, and strolled down the street.

When I knew I was safe, I took off. I ran harder than I'd ever run in any track meet. I counted the blocks as I passed. Two, three, five, ten, fifteen, twenty-two, twenty-eight. My sweater was soaked, my hair stringy and damp, when I finally stumbled into the gym. They were playing the last song as Mike shyly took my hand. We danced that one dance as if there were no yesterdays and no tomorrows.

4
Goodbye, Sweet Innocence

Those sweet songs of innocence were soon to fade. Some crucial lessons were sinking in: No one could be trusted. Trusting Mother was out of the question, and Dad—every time I tried to trust him and got close to him, he turned on me by demanding sex. Was he my friend or my enemy?

If I couldn't even trust my own parents, then who could I trust? Parents are a child's mirror of what the world outside the family unit is like. I looked in that mirror and saw strife, discord, and sexual perversion, and I began to believe that this was the way everyone was.

The other lesson I learned was in regard to power. Namely, it helped to have it. One of the surest tickets to survival was to have something someone else wanted and to be able to use it. I knew I had that kind of power over Dad. The older I got, the more I felt the force of this power. I never once chose to use it, to manipulate his feelings, to tease him or to lead him on in any way. But when he came after me, I nevertheless felt that power. It was that hard side of me, that "survival-at-all-costs" side taking over. They were teaching me that it was a dog-eat-dog world, and I was learning my lessons well.

Curiously, though, it was an old photograph which really gave me the ultimate power, the power of knowing who I was. The picture was in Mom's dresser drawer, hidden, but not too hidden, and I stared hard at the curly black hair, the dark skin, the flashing smile of the strange Mexican man who looked so familiar. Slowly, deliberately, I held the dog-eared photo next to my own face. I put us both up to the mirror, side by side. We looked like twins, he and I, like brother and sister. I had always suspected that my "new" father was not related to me, and now I knew without a doubt, that for the first time I was meeting the man who was my real father.

I didn't cry out. I didn't say anything. I just sat down on the bed and let my feelings flow. First shock. Then confusion. Then . . . then the sweet perfume of that power.

I didn't belong only to my mother, and for sure I didn't belong to that man who abused me. I belonged instead to this man, whom I already loved madly. He was my Daddy, and that made me different. I had a dark, handsome, mysterious, father who smiled back at me when I smiled at him, who loved me from that photograph. I knew if I ever met him, he would treat me as I deserved, as a father should treat a daughter.

I had found my identity in a dresser drawer, and it had set me free.

From then on, it was only a matter of time until I broke away. One Saturday, as Mother and Dad and Donna were deep into one of their lamp-throwing, name-calling free-for-alls, I couldn't stand it anymore.

"If I live in this zoo much longer, I'll turn into an animal myself," I thought. I had to get out, but where? Finally, in utter desperation, I walked the seven or eight blocks to the juvenile hall.

"I don't know how to say this, but I've gotta get in here," I told the lady behind the ancient desk. "I'd rather live in this prison than the one at home." I held my breath. She made a few phone calls and said, "Follow me, please." I was free.

"For once I'm going to have an uninterrupted night's sleep," I thought. No fear of nightmares. No fear of Dad sneaking in or Mom cussing at me in the morning. Just me and that big fluffy pillow. Already I felt more at home than I had ever felt at home.

But that night, just as I was dozing off, someone nudged me.

"Hey, sweetheart. Wake up. We're the welcoming committee, and we've got something for you."

Instantly, I was awake. I saw gray shadows looming large against the wall. I bolted up. Six girls were coming towards me.

"Hey, Miss Goody-Two-Shoes is awake. She's afraid we're out to get her."

"You broads better back up," I said, trying to sound tough. My voice quavered.

"Hey, honey, word's out you're still a virgin. We don't like virgins around here. They haven't lived," said a tall skinny one. They all laughed, and they edged closer.

"Yeah. We thought you'd like to be initiated into our exclusive society," said another one. "With this." She held up what had once been a toothbrush.

"Nobody touches me without my saying so," I said, and my voice this time sounded more like a snarl. I was surprised, but then not surprised. I had had it with people abusing me. I wasn't about to take it here.

"You girls just better back off, because I mean business," I said, and I jumped down from my bunk, grabbing a 7-Up bottle on the way.

They looked at each other.

"I said get lost, and I mean it" I broke the bottle over the steel bed frame and started towards them. I had never, never in all those years at home, been this angry. They began to back up.

"Stay and fight, you chickens. I'd love to get ahold of just one of you."

"Hey, Sue, she's serious."

"Yeah, let's beat it. She's not worth it, anyway."

They turned to leave, and that got me madder than ever.

"Hey, I'm not through with you yet. You think you can come in here and threaten me and then leave?" I slowly followed two of them down the hall.

"She's nuts," I heard one of them say, and I guess I was a little crazy, because all of a sudden I was yelling and screaming and swearing at them. All the things I had ever wanted to scream at Dad I was now screaming at them, in the language Mother had taught me. I chased them until even I knew it was useless, then ran back to my room and demolished it. Broke the flimsy lamp. Tore all the bedding to shreds. Tried to flush the 7-Up bottle down the toilet. Finally, after I could do no more damage, I slept.

About 5:00 a.m. I awoke and saw and remembered.

"Was that me?" I thought. I lay on the bed and cringed at all I had said and done, but every time I thought about anyone laying a hand on me, I got mad all over again. The room was totally ransacked.

"What got into me? I'll just have to learn to control myself," I thought. "If I want to control, I'll have to be in control." That seemed to comfort me, and when I saw the girls at breakfast and they respectfully moved over to let me sit down, I even felt rather proud of myself. I had made my point. For once it was my show. Once more I had learned a lesson in power: beating others down makes me big. It was a lesson which was to cause me endless misery in the years to follow.

I would have been perfectly happy to live at juvenile hall for a long time, but Mother and Dad came to get me about three weeks later.

"We don't want to mess with juvenile authorities," she said, "so come on home."

"You call that dump a home?"

Then Dad started in.

"Please, honey, come home. You know I love you."

"Yeah, I get that idea."

He turned his face away, and, just as I was about to leave, he did a strange thing. He started to cry. I had never seen him cry before, and I felt myself being moved.

"Oh, what's the difference?" I said, and I agreed to give it a try.

Things were never the same after that. Neither Mom nor Dad ever laid a hand on me again. Maybe I had shocked them, maybe they were afraid of the law, or maybe they could just tell a different woman had come home, one who wasn't so easily abused. Even though they left me pretty much to myself, I had had a taste of freedom and was now only in search of the right circumstances before I left again.

My chance came a few months later, in April. A girlfriend, Linda, told me in confidence that she was running away from home.

"My dad's a little too friendly when he drinks," she said.

She didn't say much more but she didn't have to.

"Here's someone I can identify with," I thought. "She knows what I've been through." We rented a hotel room, I got a job as a ticket girl in a local movie house, I packed my things, and I was gone. I didn't even look back as I slammed the door behind me.

I had just turned sixteen.

5
Wedding Bell Blues

"Freedom's just another word for nothing left to lose." It would be years before I heard Janis Joplin wail those words, but in that dingy apartment, I experienced for the first time the great high of being on my own. I felt I did have nothing left to lose; my life had been so bad up to that point that I was sure anything would have to be better. It would be years before I fully realized how relentlessly that painful past would stalk me.

Mother called shortly after I got settled.

"You better come home, Judy, or I'll make you wish you had."

"The days of threats are over, Mother. I'll live in juvenile hall before I'll live with you," I said. I hung up.

"I can't believe I did that," I thought.

I celebrated by shaving my legs and underarms. Mother had never wanted me to "grow up and look trampy" so she frowned on lipstick and shaving. I had lived in constant embarrassment whenever I was forced to raise my hand in school with a sleeveless blouse on, but no more. For a long time I raised my hand for every question, whether I knew it or not.

Clothes were another luxury I indulged in. Mother had always chosen my clothes for me—either hand-me-downs or stuff bought at thrift stores or the cheapest department stores.

"Beggars can't be choosers," she said. "I can't afford any more for you."

So I wore out-of-style, dumpy clothes, mis-matched sweater sets, scruffy saddle shoes. As an adult I can sympathize with living on a budget, but at that time it was a low blow for someone who needed so badly to be accepted in school. I felt the clothes she made me wear were visible proof of how little she cared for me. If she had shown me more love, the clothes wouldn't have mattered.

What made me even more bitter is that mother never once made any attempt to get even part-time work to help support us. To me it seemed she was just lazy, lying around the house and then complaining how poor we were. I was determined to be different. I would work hard, make my own way and give myself some of the things I'd been deprived of for so long. I would make myself look and feel special for a change.

For several months I went to school during the day and worked nights and weekends at the theater ticket office, but I was surprised that a vague sense of unhappiness stayed with me, on and on. I needed to shake my past, all of it, so in the middle of my senior year I quit school.

"High school's for kids," I said. I felt old beyond my years.

I hadn't stopped to think that saying goodbye to Los Gatos High meant saying goodbye to a way of life that had bolstered me, boosted my ego. I had taken for granted all those old memories, but now, in the stuffy hotel room during the day, I relived them with Linda.

"Remember the junior prom and how old Miss Banstrum thought we were dancing close? No wonder she never got a man."

"Yeah, Judy, and remember how the band played at the football games? And how you all strutted down the field with your batons? I always did like to watch that."

"Yeah, and the smell of popcorn in the gym? And those fierce baseball games we got into?"

"Yeah."

"And here we are stuck in a dump, with the bathroom down the hall. Who would've thought it?"

Even more frustrating was the fact that all my high school buddies envied me, the cool chick who had guts enough to junk it all and was out doing her thing while they were stuck with sentence diagrams and senioritis. I was too proud to admit my mistake, so I acted bored when they got their class rings and blasé when they passed around their yearbooks.

"You guys all excited about that kid stuff?" I yawned. Inside, I felt sick with longing.

The months passed. I worked at the theater at night and killed time during the day. Judy and Colleen were still my close friends, but they knew school would soon be out and were searching for something, too. We vaguely realized we were entering a world that seemed to have no place for us, and, like so many teenagers before us, no one had ever really warned us how scary those feelings could be.

"Hey, man, we're all washed up at sixteen," we joked. "The world's passin' us by."

But I was determined to stop that carousel, to jump on the highest horse and be noticed. I would make my own way—that's all there was to it. Or so I thought.

I was dating a lot, but "true love" always seemed to be in the next room or in that other car whizzing by. I spent hours in my room soaking up the Top 40 hits. "Love me tender, love me true/All my dreams fulfill" drifted down the dingy corridors and wove itself in and out of my dreams. Now that I was rid of Dad, I thought I had just as much chance as any other girl to find Mr. Right, and he occupied every corner of every fantasy.

He would adore me, put me on that pedestal I knew I deserved, and love me from a distance. As he proposed, he would get down on his knees and kiss my hand, his voice church-soft.

I was still believing all this when a man I'll call Tom came into my life. He was a hardwood floor layer with a big car and a steady paycheck. He was twenty-one, he treated me nicely and he wanted to marry me.

I might never have considered him except for one thing: all the while we were dating he kept his hands off me. That really impressed me. I couldn't believe anyone would love me enough not to get fresh with me. Here was someone who loved me, Judy, for being myself! The thought continually amazed me.

Still, I felt uneasy and begged him to enlist in the service to give me more time to think. But Tom didn't want Uncle Sam—he wanted me, and he gave me an engagement ring to prove it. That ring was probably what swayed me. It was something to show to my friends, something visible, a tangible sign that someone loved me enough to spend money on me, to care for me. When I was looking at it or thinking about it, I felt loved; when I thought about Tom or was with him, I got confused, so I kept my eyes on that ring.

"A diamond is forever," the ads say, but in my fantasies I didn't care about forever; I couldn't see past the church and the wedding ceremony itself. Sadly, my whole concept of what marriage entailed was centered on one figure—me, walking down that aisle. The church would be packed with all my high school friends, and Mother and Dad would sit in the front row. Finally they would be forced to come to one of my performances. They would smile at me and maybe even choke back some tears.

And they would see me in my white dress, symbol of the virginity I still had, even after all those struggles with Dad. I had earned that white dress, and I would radiate an inner glow as I floated down the aisle in it. Afterwards, there would be kisses, champagne, flashbulbs and tears, like my sister Donna had had at her wedding. On this one day, at least, we would seem to all the world like a normal family and I, the bride, would seem loved.

The date was set for June 1957, the week after all my friends graduated. Whenever I found myself getting cold feet I said, "You've got no place else to go, Judy." And I didn't.

Looking back, I see that the week of my wedding was a crucial one in my life, but for all the wrong reasons. The dress I wore was an ugly purple, not the pure white one I'd dreamed about. ("We can't afford a fancy dress for you," Mother had said, and I couldn't afford one either.) But the real shock came when I looked down the aisle: my side of the church was almost empty. Just Grandma, Judy and Colleen sat there. Dad was off gambling somewhere; Mom said later she had nothing to wear; Donna wasn't speaking to me.

"I guess everybody got mixed up as to where to sit," I joked to an usher. I was crying bitterly as I walked down the aisle, but then brides are supposed to cry, so no one said anything. The weight in my chest was like a cement block. I faced the reception and the wedding night with a broken heart—and mixed emotions.

"What do you think, Sally?" I'd asked a friend the night before.

"Are you really different after the wedding night or do you only start acting different? You know, all radiant and stuff."

"I think you are different. A man owns your body, doesn't he? And you have to give in to him and love him and do what he says. It must be so neat."

"Yeah," I said, but inside, my stomach twisted a little. I wasn't sure I wanted any man owning me, telling me what to do.

As we drove away from the church that knot inside me twisted even tighter, but it was a see-through negligee that really sealed my doom. It had seemed so shimmering and sexy at the wedding shower, but when I put it on in the fluorescent lighting of the motel bathroom, it seemed obscene. I checked myself out in the mirror and knew.

"I cannot go out there in that," I thought. "I just can't." The nightgown left nothing to the imagination. I would not parade in front of that man with every bit of me showing.

By this time Tom was knocking gently at the bathroom door.

"Judy, honey, are you OK? What's taking you so long?"

I couldn't answer. The idea of him out there waiting for me made me weak-kneed. I didn't even know this man, and now I was his forever? How had I gotten into this mess?

I sat down on the edge of the tub, trying to scrounge up some strategy—anything. How far was it from the bathroom door to the bed? Could I make a wild dash for it?

"Judy, come on out, honey. I won't hurt you." His voice was more insistent this time, tinged with a little annoyance.

I burrowed into some towels to keep warm while I thought. My mind was racing wildly, but no answers were coming.

"Judy, for Pete's sake, are you going to stay in there all night?" This one was sort of a whimper, but it gave me the idea I'd been searching for. I would stay in there all night. What right did he have to try to make me do something I didn't want to do?

Happily, I took those towels and carefully made up a bed for myself in the bathtub. I've never been so neat in my life—a corner tucked in here, an edge smoothed down there, and Tom banging on the door with an "I-don't-believe-this-is-happening" tone in his voice.

The bathtub was strangely comfortable that night, considering the alternative, and I slept well. I was living on my own terms.

The next morning my bleary-eyed husband and I had a talk. I was feeling sheepish and foolish, and, in the bright daylight where I was safe, I felt sorry for him.

"Tom, I'm so embarrassed. I don't know what got into me, and I'm going to try real hard to cooperate." I was serious. He was a human being, too, and marriage meant sharing, didn't it? I was really ashamed.

Even then, it took me four days and nights to get up my courage. I felt truly sorry for Tom, but I was so afraid it would be ugly, like it had been with Dad, that I was almost paralyzed. This marriage was my new start in life, and if it turned out to be just a repeat of the past, where was I then?

Finally I knew it had to be done. Although I didn't have a lot of deep feelings for my new husband, I realized that fair was fair. He wasn't getting his money's worth.

All that day I worked at trying to feel romantic. I wanted it to be special, to make me feel special. Subconsciously, I was asking this man to erase ten years of pain he didn't even know existed, but the unfairness of that didn't strike me. All I knew was that I wanted him to say, "Thank you, Judy, for saving yourself for me. I will always put you on a pedestal."

I never heard those words; I never felt I was on a pedestal.

I felt nothing.

My only reaction after it was all over was extreme bitterness.

"Is this all there is?" I asked myself. "Is this what I saved myself for?"

I had lost my last illusion.

6
The Unforgivable Sin

When I think back on my life, on all the lurid, ugly details of it before I became a Christian, there is one part, above all, that pains me like no other. I can hardly mention it or even think about it without tearing myself up inside. Every time I think of it, I flinch.

It began in a doctor's office, four months after our marriage.

"Judy, you're pregnant," our family doctor said, and my heart sunk. I smiled and acted happy, like I thought I was supposed to do, but inside all I could think was, "I need someone to take care of me, not someone for me to take care of."

When our first son was born, we named him Chuck.

I loved him. Oh, did I love him.

I held him all day and whispered to him in the night, cooing sounds, promises that he'd never feel any of the hurt I'd felt. His birth gave me a new birth, and for a while I became that soft little child of five who was still on the farm, still surrounded by love and able to give that love to others. But all the tenderness I felt didn't hide the fact that, at seventeen, I was a child trying to raise another child. The strain of this tore at the marriage.

At first I didn't know what was bugging me. I would make mental lists of Tom's good points, trying to talk myself into loving him.

"He treats me nicely. He provides well for me. He always comes home at night. He doesn't mess around or go out with the boys. What more do I want?"

But there was so much missing, and I knew it. All my life I had dreamed of that Prince Charming who would whisk me away to some place where I could forget the past, where I could regain the happiness I'd known those first five years.

I needed a lifetime of love, free and unconditional, in order to feel good about myself, but at that time I didn't understand any of this. All I knew was that my past was still haunting me. The worst part was the sex: I didn't want any part of it. We'd lie in bed at night, far apart.

"Judy, what's wrong with you? Why are you so nervous all the time? I won't hurt you," he would say.

"I don't know, Tom. I guess I just can't concentrate. My mind is always going."

"Well, just think of me, honey. That should help you concentrate." And he'd snuggle even closer. Then I'd pray for Chuckie to cry, for anything. I couldn't help thinking about Dad all those times. After spending so many years under his control, it was almost driving me crazy to be under Tom's control. Every time Tom came near me, he seemed like Dad to me, and I was completely repulsed and blindingly mad.

"This is my husband," I kept telling myself. "He has a right to be demanding." But when I closed my eyes, he became Dad again. It was awful, and neither of us could figure out what was wrong. I didn't dare to think it, but deep in my mind, I knew I wanted out. Too late, I realized I had gotten married for all the wrong reasons, and since no one had ever raised me to believe marriage was a lifetime commitment, I could see it only as a trap.

My restlessness got so obvious it was like a third person in our marriage, a looming force that sat at every meal with us and lay down between us at night.

"What you need is another baby, honey," said Tom, and four months later, despite my own precautions, I was pregnant again. I was sick all during that pregnancy, both physically and emotionally, but when Gary was born, that love flowed through me once more.

"How can I have two such beautiful sons?" I wondered. Once again, that well of love deep inside me had been tapped.

AUG 1960

Chuckie — 3 yrs old   Gary — 2 yrs old

Tom bought us a new house in the suburbs, and, for the first and last time in my life, I fell into a lifestyle that could be called typically American. I scrubbed floors. I changed diapers. I walked the babies and nodded at the neighbors. I changed more diapers. I had a hot meal on the table when Tom came home at six.

But I had no friends, and I was bored senseless. I watched the soaps on TV and wondered how all those women could seem so interested in their drab lives. Who cared if the toilet bowl was dirty? So what if the glasses had water spots on them? Did people actually dedicate the best years of their lives to discussing bleaches and washing spit-up out of their blouses?

"Where is the happiness in life?" I wondered. "Does everybody live this way?" The commercials showed tan young people sailing, laughing, drinking beer and singing by open fires. I couldn't understand who those people were and how they had gotten there. When would it be my turn to sing?

"Maybe I should try harder to love Tom, to do things his way," I thought, so I tried that, but it was almost impossible after all those "Someday you'll be in control" promises I'd made to myself.

"Maybe life doesn't offer any more happiness than this," I thought. I didn't know.

The months plodded by uneventfully, dutifully, one after another in a steady, monotonous pace. We began fighting, and the fights got worse. Neither of us knew who we were or what we were doing or what we wanted, and all the while there were the two babies, clinging, hanging, dependent.

In all, we stuck together for over two years. We would fight, I'd pack and leave, one child under each arm. He'd call. I'd come back. We'd fight again, and the cycle would start all over. Finally, one day, I just didn't come back. With both boys still in diapers, I had decided to go it alone.

Tom called me at a girlfriend's house.

"I want you back, Judy. We're a family, and we should stay a family."

"It's no good, Tom, can't you see that? We're both grinding each other to dust."

"I'll buy you something, anything you want. You name it."

"All you men are alike. You all think love is for sale, that you can buy it and use it and then throw it away." I was yelling at him now.

"Okay, then, have it your way, but you and the boys will never see a red cent of mine, not if you're not living under my roof." His voice was shaking, and he slammed the phone in my ear.

"Goodbye, Tom," I said, and then I cried. Where did I go with two babies, no money and no job?

But after the tears stopped, I felt a little better.

"I'm free, and nobody's ever going to trap me again. From now on, it's my way or no way." I was hardening myself for the trouble I knew was ahead; that was the only way I knew to face things. Just grit your teeth, tell yourself nothing bothered you, and set out to conquer the world. I thought there was nobody to rely on except myself, but I can see now that it was that attitude, that "me-against-the-world" feeling, more than anything else, which led me even deeper into my years of pain.

Again, I moved into an apartment and began what I hoped was a fresh life. I got a job in a steak house at night, so I could be with the kids during the day. The meal I had at work was usually the only food I ate all day. I made big pots of spaghetti for the boys and they would eat it while I watched. One by one, I hocked my appliances for a little extra cash here and there.

I began dating a little bit and trying to enjoy my new-found freedom, but my money worries and problems with the kids kept getting me down. I was only nineteen, but I felt sometimes like ninety compared to the teen-aged crowd I hung around with. I was going through one job after another—waitress in a donut shop, car hop, brussel's sprout sorter. That last one was the pits for me. All night I stood at a conveyor belt, weeding out the bad brussels sprouts from the bunch. When I got hungry enough, I ate them.

"I can't believe it's come to this," I thought.

Finally, after about ten months of desperation, I went to a social agency. Both babies were with me, crying and fighting, but still the lady at the desk wouldn't look up. At last, her head buried in important papers, she said, "And I suppose you're here for welfare?"

"Ma'am, I don't know. I just need help. Somebody to talk to, or something."

"Well, you'll have to wait your turn, you know. And I'd appreciate it if next time you don't bring those babies. This is serious business here."

I waited. The kids screamed and then slept.

Finally she said, "Well, you might as well fill out these forms while you're waiting."

There were a lot of them. I glanced at the clock. It was almost 4:25. I'd been there for over two hours.

"You'd better hurry. We close at five on the dot."

At 4:50, I handed her all the papers.

"Why you should've spoken up, girl," she said after a brief glance at the top line. "You should've told me you were still married. We could've both saved ourselves a lot of time."

"But we're separated, my husband and me. I don't want anything from him, and he swore he wouldn't give me a penny anyway. Not unless I come back to him."

"I don't know what it is about you young girls these days. Think you're too good to stick a marriage out like the rest of us did. The state can't give you anything, honey, not while your husband makes good money. We're not in the business of supporting girls who cry every time they have to wash a dish."

"Well, where am I going to go, then?" I hated myself for asking, but her agency was my last hope.

"Why not back with your husband where you belong? It won't be so hard. Just tell him your little experiment was a mistake, that's all. You'll see. You'll both forget it in no time."

Her head was back in the papers. Outside, about a block away, I sat on the curb, with both babies hanging onto me, and cried.

"What happens to people when they're down and out? Who helps them?" I wondered. When the kids heard me crying, they cried, too, and we all three sat there, bawling, for a long time.

My mind got a little strange after that. In the market I saw all sorts of people spending money on luxuries like suntan oil and toys and liquor and magazines, and they plopped their ten and twenty dollar bills on the counter without a trace of emotion.

"Where do they get all that money?" I wondered. "Why don't I have any?"

But my money worries, as gigantic as they were, were nothing compared to my fears for the babies. I worried about them constantly; their sitters weren't taking good care of them. They weren't eating right. They were feeling my tension and troubles. They were cooped up in an apartment, living with a crabby mother who worked all night and got no sleep all day. I loved them, and yet I was failing as a mother and was dragging them down with me. My sons, my beautiful sons.

Finally, one day something happened which convinced me I would have to take drastic action. I awoke to a too-quiet house, and, in a growing panic, realized the alarm read 10 o'clock. Ten o'clock! Where were the kids? I stumbled and crashed my way into the living room. The front door was wide open, and the chair I usually barred it with was overturned.

I can still see today what I saw out that door. There, in the middle of the highway in front of the apartment, was three-year-old Chuckie on his tricycle. Traffic was stalled for two miles each way, and my son was leading the parade. I knew then that I could no longer go on taking care of them, at least not under those circumstances. It would be only a matter of time before something drastic happened to us all.

For several sleepless nights I racked my brain, trying to find a way out, and that's when my thinking started getting messed up. That's where I made my mistake. I started to feel that if only the boys weren't always underfoot, I'd be okay.

"I need someone to take the kids for a month or so until I sort things out, get back on my feet," I thought. "I have to be free to think, to plan."

There seemed to be no one around to take them.

Teen-aged sitters were out; they were in school most of the day, anyway. I didn't want or trust a grown woman in the apartment. Besides, there wasn't enough room for that. As hard as I thought, there was only one person I could come up with. My mother. She had moved back to Oklahoma and was babysitting Donna's kids full time. Maybe she'd watch mine for a few weeks, too.

"Don't do it, Judy," my conscience kept telling me. "You were miserable there. They would be, too."

"But Mom's mellowed in her old age," I argued, and it was true. The older I got, the nicer she seemed. "Besides, they're boys. Dad wouldn't be after them, and he could take them hunting and stuff. He's a great guy as long as sex isn't involved."

This mental battle must have gone on for at least a week. I'd pick up the phone to call and hang it back up again a dozen times a day. I kept struggling on, but it was just too hard. Sitters' fees were eating up my measly paycheck, and the boys were really beginning to suffer. Finally, I hit on the idea that I would send only Chuckie.

"I'll keep the baby with me," I thought. "He needs me the most." I mistakenly assumed that at three, Chuckie would be better able to adjust to change than Gary, who was not quite two.

I called Mother.

"You know I got my hands full with Donna's kids," she said, "but if you can send me some money, I'll do it."

"I'll send you all I can, I promise." Already I was feeling guilty and was trying to buy those feelings away.

"Nobody can say you haven't tried," I comforted myself as I hung up the phone.

I looked then at that little three-year-old, with his cowlick and his chubby wrists, and felt a stab of pain that took my breath away. I didn't know how I would stand putting him on that plane. For the next couple of days I held him and rocked him and sang to him almost constantly. I memorized the sound of his voice and studied hard the way he walked.

"Chuckie, Chuckie, baby, you'll come back to Mama soon," I said.

"I'm not going, Mama. I'm staying with you and brother."

Finally the day came. I left Gary with a sitter, and

Chuckie and I began the long bus ride to the airport. I didn't have enough money for a round-trip ticket for me to go along, so I bought a full-fare ticket with the agreement that a stewardess would take special care of him and make sure he got there safely.

There aren't any words I know that I can use to describe how I felt that day when I left him, seat belt fastened, on that plane. Today I would starve first before I would send a child of mine away, but then I was young, I was foolish, and I was scared. The future was like a room whose walls were closing in on me. I had to get out before I suffocated. I had to do what I thought was right at the moment and let later worry about later.

But for months after that, I saw him sitting there, dwarfed by that huge seat, little legs jutting straight out in front of him. I kissed him all over, and my tears slid down his new shirt.

"You'll have fun at Grandma's, honey," I said. "You will, you will."

I patted his slicked-down hair, trying not to glance at his little face. He knew something was going on, but he couldn't figure out what. His big eyes were filling with tears.

"Mama, where are you going? Mama?" I kissed him once more and tried to tighten his seat belt, but I was so choked up I could hardly breathe. His arms were around my neck like a vise. Should I keep him?

"You'll have to go now, Miss," a stewardess said. Without thinking, I pried away the chubby arms, turned around and ran down the aisle as fast as I could.

"Mama! Come back! Don't leave me! Mama!" He was screaming now, and my head was pounding, but then the engines started roaring, and I couldn't hear a thing. I ran down the steps, through the terminal, across the parking lot and to the bus stop. My chest felt like someone was snuffing out my life from the inside.

What had I done?

I came home to a lonely house and sat, waiting for Mother to call.

"Judy, he got here okay, but he's hysterical," she said. "He's screaming and crying for you, and no one can comfort him. He doesn't know who we are."

Those words hurt, hurt bad, but then she said something that made me mad.

"You can't take a little kid from his mother and put him with strangers. What's wrong with you, anyway?"

How dare she tell me how to raise children! Of all people! I was so mad that I didn't let myself think about Chuckie. The nerve of her!

That was the first time I can remember that I got angry at someone else to avoid my own guilt, but it wasn't to be the last. In fact, I know now that sending Chuckie away was a turning point in my life, for everything that happened to me afterwards was an effort to cover up and forget about what I had done to my son. I had made my first adult decision, and I had blown it in every way.

It's too hard, even now, to describe what the next month was like. I couldn't sleep, I couldn't eat, I couldn't get any peace. I knew that I should've hopped on the next plane to rescue him, but I didn't, and I didn't want to think why. Inside of me, I felt I just couldn't make it with both kids, yet I knew other people did, and that thought killed me.

I must've called every other night to check on him. A couple of times I tried talking to him, but that was impossible for both of us. As soon as he heard my voice, he cried and screamed for me and begged me to come and get him. Then, for days afterwards, he wouldn't eat or sleep. Mother was about at her wit's end, and so was I.

Just as I was wrestling with what to do about everything, MaRue and Ardean called. They had been in touch with me off and on through the years, and when they heard a son of mine was visiting Mom, they couldn't wait to see him. They were shocked at what they saw.

"Judy, that child is pathetic," they said. "He just sits in a dark room and stares. He's so lonely. Let us take him and raise him. You know we'll give him a good home."

Visions of fireplaces roaring and pies baking came

rushing back to me, and I made a second mistake. I told myself they were right. If I let him live with them, I rationalized, I could still keep those promises I'd made to him when he was born; he would have the childhood I had always wanted. He could feed the chickens and count the stars and join the Boy Scouts and go to Sunday school—all the things I had dreamed about for myself for so long. All the things I could never give him.

Best of all, I thought, he would be loved. What better sacrifice could I make for my son than to let him be loved?

But MaRue and Ardean attached one condition: I must promise never to come and take him away the way Mother had taken me away from them.

"We just won't go through that kind of hurt again, Judy," they said. "You can understand that."

I thought hard for a few days, but, looking back, I know now that the real decision had been made when I put him on the plane. Finally, I gave them my permission.

"I think you've made the right choice, Judy," MaRue told me. "You know how we want children. And you can visit any time, you know that. We still love you so much, and when you and Gary come it'll be just like a big family reunion."

"Oh Mom MaRue, I'll start saving up right now. I can visit at Christmas and on holidays, and when Chuckie gets older I can tell him why I did all this. He'll have such a good life there, and I know someday he'll thank me for it."

But in the nighttime, alone, on those nights when I couldn't sleep, I would always hear the roar of the jet engine and that little voice crying, "Mama! Don't leave me."

On those nights, I cried my bitterest tears, not only for that little three-year-old, but for a five-year-old girl who, so long ago, had grown up alone in a house full of strangers.

I had condemned him to relive a part of my past, and the weight of that decision hung around my neck, like a millstone, for years and years and years.

7
Rip Off

It wasn't long after Chuckie moved to the farm that I began to look for a new home for Gary, too.

"I can't believe it," I told a friend. "One baby ties me down as much as two ever did. I need to come and go at all hours, or I'll never make a decent living."

This was one part truth and three parts rationalization, but, as I pushed the guilt about Chuckie farther back in my mind, it became easier for me to do the same about Gary. It wasn't long before Mrs. Moody, a grandmotherly lady with arms just made for hugging kids, offered to keep Gary in her home across town.

"How perfect," I thought. "I can visit him every night after work and on weekends, and I won't always have to be carting him from one sitter to the next. Kids need consistency." So Gary and his diapers and his toys moved in with "Mama" Moody for awhile. Part of me missed him, but the other part of me felt vastly relieved.

"Free at last!" I thought. "I'm on my own! No more husband or kids to tie me down, no Dad and Mom to make me feel bad, no one to think of but myself!" The first few weeks were fantastic. I was a kid on summer vacation, a convict just paroled. I started to hang around the discotheques in Santa Cruz, dancing all night and sleeping late in the mornings. To my mind, I was really living high.

I also started drinking in those clubs. Not a lot at first, just more than I ever thought I would. I didn't know it then, but I know it now: I was slowly constructing my own private prison in those years, just as surely as if I were laying each brick myself. My guilt over the things I'd done with Dad had been bad enough, but now I had added to it crimes against my own children. Up until that time, I had been somewhat the victim, the person "sinned" against, but when I pushed the kids out of my life, they became the victims and I the "sinner." Somewhere, on some level, I knew this, and from that time on, I guess, I just couldn't face myself. I was doomed to turn the other way and run, and what better way than through booze and good times?

So I adopted the "Playboy" philosophy. Do anything you want as long as it doesn't hurt anyone else, and that "anything" began to include going to bed with guys I really liked. But even then, it wasn't that neat; I'd be attracted to them until we hit the sack. Then I would be sick of them and refuse to see them again. I was proud of all this independence. The louder the music got, the faster the dancing became, the happier I thought I was.

Yet every time I heard a kid call "Mama," I knew it was for me. I'd turn around, heart pounding, but no one was ever there. I was still phoning Chuckie every week until finally MaRue begged me to quit.

"He misses you too much, Judy. Every time he hears your voice he falls apart. If you love him you'll stop calling him for awhile."

I did love him, so I quit calling. At night I would lie awake and have imaginary conversations with him, telling him about my day and asking him about his. But then I'd catch myself.

"Don't be such a sap. The kid's better off without you. What kind of lifestyle would this be for a three-year old? You aren't exactly the Sunday school type, you know."

I got to see Gary every weekend, though. His new home across town was a comfortable one, and whenever I felt bad about him living there, I'd compare that house to my dinky apartment.

"My sons are being raised in the style I wish I'd been accustomed to," I joked to my friends.

Gary was pretty young at the time and seemed to be adjusting better than Chuckie was. Still, he would wait for me on the front steps, much as I had waited for my Grandma years ago, and when he saw me coming, he'd yell "Mommy! Mommy!" and tear down the street towards me. We'd have a great visit (I was spending half my paycheck on toys for him) but I always dreaded leaving him because he would always cry and hang onto me.

"When you coming back, Mommy? Do I have to live here long?"

"We'll see, honey. We'll talk about it next time." Then I'd go home and worry about what I was going to say when "next time" came around. As it turned out, the problem took care of itself. After a few months, he stopped asking me and seemed to fade into the background when leave-taking time came around. Soon he didn't even bother to say goodbye. As usual, I was a little slow in catching on, until one Sunday, at a neighborhood playground, he hung by his knees from the jungle gym and said, "Look, Judy! Won't Mama be proud?"

I had lost him. He had transferred his love for me to another woman, and that night, under the pretense of celebrating how happy my two sons were, I got very, very drunk. From then on, his living there, which had started out as a temporary convenience, stretched out into a permanent arrangement. After a time, it even seemed natural that he should be living with Mrs. Moody instead of with me.

I was to spend the next eleven years looking for meaning in my life, yet I had just given up a woman's most meaningful blessings, her children.

I hit the clubs every night after that, and it was at about this time that I began hearing about a fantastic musician appearing at the Beachcomber.

"This guy has the world's greatest personality," my friend Laurie told me. "He is one of those people who just loves everybody."

"Oh? What's his name?"

"Jimmy Mamou."

All my girlfriends had crushes on him, so, of course, I had to go in there and check him out. It's funny now, to think back on those first impressions of the man I was to share my life with. I had heard so much good about him that I was determined not to like him. And I didn't, at least not at first.

"His music's great, but don't you think he comes on a little strong?" I asked. The thing was, I just couldn't believe he was for real. He was too nice—the kind of guy who likes everyone equally, who makes every woman feel she is the only person in the room.

"You actually gonna fall for that syrupy line of his?" I kidded my friends. "You might've been born yesterday, but not me. Count me out."

But every time I went in there he made a special point to talk to me, to notice especially me.

"I like your hair that way, Judy," he'd say whenever I changed my hair style, or "I haven't seen that dress before. Is it new?"

"I can't believe I'm falling for this," I thought, and it irritated me a little. Was he out for what he could get, or wasn't he? My past had conditioned me to believe that everybody had to have a gimmick. What was his? Somehow, though, I found myself dancing to his music more and more often. Soon I began turning down dates just to watch him play.

"You can like him, but never trust him," I told myself, and the nicer he was to me, the more I was torn between letting my guard down and keeping it up. Probably, had I allowed the side of me that wanted to trust him to take over, I might have married him and lived happily ever after, but the harder, more practical side of me kept intervening. So it was that one night, right in front of my future husband's eyes, I inadvertently had my first brush with what was later to turn into a career of prostitution.

I was sitting at the bar, losing myself in Jimmy's music, when a dark Latin-type man walked up to me and said, "How much would it cost to go to bed with you?" Lots of men had kidded with me about going to bed, but this was the first time a man had attached a price to it.

"How much you got?" I said, stringing him along for the fun of it.

He handed me his wallet, and I counted seven big bills.

"That's twice what I make in a week at the bakery!" I thought. I really couldn't believe that it was possible for me to make two weeks' wages in just one hour. I didn't feel much like making love to him, but I was definitely interested in that money. Besides, I told myself, it couldn't be any worse than what I'd done with Dad.

"You're on; mister," I said.

He put his arm around me possessively and pushed me toward the door. My mind was going faster than a buzz saw. Was I really going to go through with this? As we drove out of the parking lot, I took a better look at him. He was fairly good-looking, a clean-cut man in his mid-thirties. Nothing special. "Mr. Average," I thought.

"Hey, can I ask you something silly? What are you doing this for?" I said. This whole thing was so weird to me, and I needed to come to grips with it.

"Cause you look good to me, honey, and I like having what I want."

I didn't like that too much. Did the guy think he owned me or something? "But what about your wife? Are you from out of town or something?

He stiffened a bit when I mentioned her, but I didn't care. Somehow, it was important for me to know.

"Kid, if you're so curious, she's about a mile-and-a-half down the road waiting for me to come home from my weekly gin game." He laughed at this, like he was pulling something over on somebody.

"But don't you love her?"

"Love her?" He seemed surprised. "Yeah, yeah, I guess I do. Yeah, she's all right. Hey, let's cut the chatter and figure out where we're going, OK? I ain't got all night."

I knew now I wouldn't be caught dead in bed with him. Why should I? He was just a dirty old man like Dad, all wound up in his own stupid passions and not caring about anybody else but himself. His poor wife, sitting there waiting for him to come home . . . he needed to know that men don't own women, can't automatically possess them whenever they want. He needed somebody to teach him a lesson, the creep.

I decided to ditch him. He was half drunk already, so I told him I needed some booze to get me more in the mood, hoping he'd go into the liquor store alone and I could make a run for it. As he got out of the car, he said in this supposedly neat voice, "Don't go 'way, baby. You've got a real treat in store for you."

I couldn't believe it. That fool. I scooted across the seat, and as I got out of the car, something dropped to the ground. His wallet! He had left his wallet in the car with most of the money inside.

I was running on pure reflex now, pure adrenalin, as I pocketed the money, revved up the engine and squealed the car around. I could see him through the liquor store window and, on impulse, I honked and waved. The look of shock and anger on his face had an unexpected effect on me: it scared me, but I also felt a mighty surge of power. Of superb, outlandish joy. I had ripped him off before he could touch me! I had shown him, him and all the men like him what it felt like to be used.

"You deserve every bit of it, sucker," I chuckled, and I started laughing so hard I could barely see to drive. I parked the car a few blocks away, where he'd be sure to find it, and ran all the way home, laughing so hard my sides hurt. It was pathetic how funny the whole thing struck me. I lay awake almost all night, patting myself on the back and planning how to spend that fortune.

The next morning, when I woke up, it didn't seem quite so hilarious.

"You stole that man's money," I told myself.

"Are you kidding?" I answered back. "If he's lucky maybe he learned a lesson: if you're going to cheat, expect to get cheated on."

Still, all day my eyes avoided that wallet sitting on top of the dresser.

Around eleven, I went to get my car, and, as I pulled away from the Beachcomber, I saw him waiting for me across the parking lot.

"Oh, God help me!" I thought. He was mad.

I took off and he took off after me, up on sidewalks, into trash cans, down the wrong side of streets, through narrow alleys. I was petrified. I knew if he ever caught me he would kill me.

At the first chance, I screeched up to a gas station and yelled to the owner, "Call the police. A crazy man is trying to molest me!"

By the time he pulled up to me, the police had pulled up, too. I drove away shaking, and spent the rest of the day nursing a migraine headache. I was getting more and more sorry about what I had done.

I drove home to Los Gatos the next day and took a temporary leave from my bakery job. I didn't ask myself why, or how I was going to support myself, I just did it. When my money was almost gone, I made my way back up to Santa Cruz, taking along my best clothes and a new wig I had bought.

"What you all dressed up for, babe?" Jimmy said when I came into the Beachcomber.

"Oh, I don't know. Just waiting to see what develops, I guess." And that was the truth. I didn't really decide what I was going to do, I just let it happen. Sure enough, the men practically fell all over me when I sent out signals I was "available."

I was a little nervous at first, but the man who picked me up that night was easier to rip off than the man the week before had been. And this time, I didn't let my conscience get the upper hand.

After a couple of nights, I had more money than I was used to seeing in a month. It was so simple, I couldn't believe it was happening. Why had I busted my brains working when I could play and get this kind of dough?

As I was driving back down the coast that night, my conscience started in on me again.

"You know what you're doing? You're cheating and stealing."

"Don't be stupid," I answered back. "I'm just teaching them a lesson. Maybe after this they'll stay home with their wives where they belong. Besides, that's what your Daddy taught you—when the world threatens, use what little power you have."

But what I didn't and couldn't admit to myself is that I enjoyed ripping these guys off, not only for the money, but for the feeling it gave me. For so many years, I had been the helpless one, the one with no power. Now I was showing these men how it felt to have the tables turned. And, to me, it felt good. Really good.

Looking back I can see that this was a crucial step in my hardening process; when I gave the kids away I had decided it was "me first," and now I had taken one more step. I was living by that code. Once again, I had a choice to make, and I chose wrongly. Mother had taught me the need to survive, and Dad had taught me the way, but I, I was the one who decided to follow that path.

"This is just a game," I kept telling myself. "Soon I'll have to go back to work again." But once I saw what kind of money I could make, I started taking it more seriously. I began stalking my prey and got really picky, choosing only well-dressed men with rings on. I'd watch them until they opened their wallets, and I got so good at this that I could tell how much they had on them even if I was sitting on the other end of a dark bar. After they had a few drinks, I'd bribe the bartender or the cocktail waitress to send them my way.

"How much, honey?" they'd say.

The rest was like taking candy from babies, except for one thing: babies are innocent, and you feel terrible when you hurt them. These men thought that just opening their wallets gave them the right to touch me, to caress me and make me do whatever they wanted. I wanted every one of them to suffer, to think twice about what they were doing before they made me or any other woman submit to them again. The bitterness I'd harbored for so many years came cascading out with a force no one could ever have predicted.

For six months or so I lived this way, feeling really high on all my independence, and getting more and more calloused about what I was doing. More and more I was suppressing anything soft and gentle in me and allowing those things hard and bitter to surface. These were such crucial months; if only I could relive them and do them differently!

But one good thing was happening—I was getting more deeply involved with Jimmy. To me, he wasn't the kind of man those men were or Dad had been, He was just Jimmy, kind, loving, easy-going, with a real ability to care for others more than he cared for himself. Although he lived the fairly wild and uninhabited life of a musician, he didn't seem a part of that rat race I despised. He seemed above it, like some kind of innocent spirit living among thieves, yet never resorting to thievery, never even being touched by it.

Once, in a serious moment, I asked him about this, about what made him different from everybody else at the clubs.

"Honey, I'm just the same as all the other guys. I like a good time, too. But I'll tell you something. I love my music."

After that I watched him even more closely. The other guys in the band, they were on ego-trips as they played. The centers of attention. Stars. Jimmy—he was into the music, floating high on his notes and nothing else. Through those feelings he seemed to rise above the wreckage people made of their lives. Once I found this out, there was no stopping my feelings for him. He didn't know how I made my living, and around him I felt like a different person, a little innocent girl again. It was he who kept alive my ability to love, to feel, and to be human.

Whenever Jimmy came up in any of our gang's conversation, somebody always said, "Oh, Jimmy. Everybody loves Jimmy." And I did, too.

But the die had been cast. I now loved money more. And power. And being on my own. I trusted Jimmy more than I trusted anyone, but I trusted myself most of all. How ironic that this trust, this self-confidence which I thought would save me, was, in the end, my undoing.

I could've lived this way a long time, making money, spending it, lulling myself to sleep to Jimmy's melodies, but around November of that year I began to feel something was different about me. I just didn't feel the same, have the same energy. All I wanted to do was sleep.

"Go to the doctor," everyone said. They were tired of my complaining. I refused. One night in a club I blacked out on the dance floor. The kindly old doctor they took me to told me what I'd known for a couple of months but had refused to admit: "Judy, you're pregnant."

I just sat there. I had been sleeping with a few boyfriends, but I didn't know who the baby's father was, and I didn't want to know.

"Do you have any relatives around, anyone who can help you?" the doctor asked.

"No. I don't have anybody."

"Do you want the baby?"

One look answered that.

He crossed the room, wrote something on a prescription pad, and handed it to me. A phone number and the words "six o'clock."

"Call and say you're hemorrhaging," he said.

8
Abortion

All day I paced the apartment.

"I'm pregnant. I can't believe it. There's a baby growing inside me, a new life. A heart beating. Arms and legs growing."

"There's no baby in there," that other voice told me. "Just a lump of chemicals, a big mass of nothing." I'd go back and forth in my mind, back and forth. Then I'd end up crying and missing Chuckie and Gary. I thought of those two boys all day—about how much I loved them. About how I'd blown it. Finally, I made the fateful decision.

"You're not motherhood material, Judy. This kid is better off not even coming into this rotten world. No use dragging him down, too." I had chosen death over life.

At six I called the number.

"Please tell the doctor it's Judy, and I'm bleeding really hard."

"Be at my office in ten minutes," said the voice. To my

surprise, it was the old doctor from this morning. Somehow he didn't seem the type.

I got there before he did and waited, shivering in the cold. "It'll be over in half an hour," I kept telling myself. "In half an hour you can walk out of here and buy a beer at the Beachcomber."

He opened the door from the inside.

"Hurry up, hurry up. You never know who's watching," he said, as he pulled me in. He didn't seem quite as nice as he had that morning, and I could've used some sympathy.

"Oh, well, I'm paying him to take care of me, not to approve of me," I thought.

The doctor sat down in his big overstuffed chair, the same one he had talked to me from that morning, but this time, something seemed different.

"I think we need to have a little chat first," he said slowly. "Yes, I think that would be in order." He seemed happy, or self-satisfied or something. I couldn't put my finger on it, but I didn't like it. I decided to play it tough, to bluff my way through.

"Look, Doc, let's just skip the counseling bit, OK? I did it, I'm sorry, I won't do it again, but now let's just get it over with, all right?"

"Well," he paused. "Well, well! We have a little lady who's in a hurry here, do we? But I'll bet she wasn't in such a hurry when she got herself into this mess, was she now? Unfortunately, Miss, in this office it's not quite as easy as one-two-three. In this office we work under somewhat of a handicap, I'm sorry to say." My heart skipped over itself.

"I've got more money if that's what you're after."

"Money? Oh no, my dear. It isn't just a question of money. It's a little matter of the proper anesthetic. You see, you're almost five months pregnant, and it's too risky, entirely too risky, to use the conventional anesthetic on you. In fact, we just might have to go it cold turkey, if you know what I mean."

He was smiling now. I just sat there.

"Well, what do you say? You're a big brave girl, aren't

you? Well built. Nice strong body. Yes, nice body. You can
take a little pain, can't you? After all that pleasure you've had,
you can stand a little pain, I think."

I remember the room started to spin as I tried hard to
focus my eyes. What was this guy's game? Before I could
think or do anything else, he took me by the arm and led me
across the room to a door.

"First we need to examine you," he said as he opened it.
When I saw what was inside, my legs buckled. A roaring
fireplace. A bearskin rug. Medical instruments reflecting from
the mirrored ceiling. A wave of nausea swept over me, and I
fell or collapsed onto a white-sheeted examination table. How
degraded everything had gotten! I was trying to clear my head
when I heard the door lock behind me.

"Be calm, Judy, be calm," I kept telling myself. "You've
been in worse situations before and you've always gotten out.
Just keep your cool this time, and you'll get out of this one,
too."

I was panicky, but I started considering my options,
limited though they were. I did want that abortion, and I had
come this far. This old guy was definitely on some weird trip,
but if I just kept my head, maybe I could outlast him. It was
already 6:15. He would have to let his guard down sometime.
Meanwhile, the only way I would be able to stand him would
be to act like I had with Dad—be a robot, think of things far
away, let him do what he wanted, and then get out of there.

It's hard for me now to talk about that night and how
shameful it was. He started out with a "pain test," beating my
bottom and back with a long, wire-bristled brush until blisters
formed. He would hit me so hard that he'd work up a sweat
and have to sit down and rest. I just lay there, tears rolling
down my cheeks. He was working too hard to talk, and I was
determined not to make a sound, so the room was quiet, except for the sounds of the beating.

I don't know how I stood all this, and it seemed almost
unbelievable to me that it was 7:25 when he told me to put on
a robe and get ready for an examination. That was almost
worse than the beatings, and I was sick with anger and revul-

sion. All the while he kept talking about how we all had to pay for everything in life, and nothing was free, that pain must follow pleasure as night follows the day.

Finally, I started crying, huge racking sobs for myself and the whole lousy world. I did have a lot to pay for, I thought. Who was I to call him sick when I had just spent the last six months of my life inflicting pain on others? Who could say what I had done to those men was any less painful in its own way than what the doctor was doing to me? I felt totally enveloped by guilt.

"We're all lost," I thought. "We're our own worst enemies, all grabbing and pushing and pulling each other down, down to the place where there is no human spirit, no loving kindness." That moment was the lowest of the low for me; I was in total despair, for myself and for the rest of the world, and self-destructive enough to let him do whatever he wanted to. I just didn't care anymore. But finally, something in him seemed old and worn out, too.

"Let's get on with it," he sighed. He, too, was beaten by that aura of evil that hung heavy in the room.

"The abortion," I thought. "Finally, the abortion." I had hung on.

"Judy." His voice was very tired now. "Judy, I wasn't lying to you before. I don't have any anesthetic here, so it will hurt a lot. But I've done it before, and I'll do it again, and somehow we survive. We all survive."

"Just get going," I said. I was so tired of him, of everything.

"I'm going to scrape the baby out of your uterus, and I'll have to do it three times to be sure," he said.

That didn't sound too bad when he said it. It was just little noises we call "words" which we all make to each other to try to convey a reality, but, oh, let me tell you, those words had nothing to do with the reality itself. No sounds I can make now, no markings on paper can let you know how much that hurt, like a giant razor cutting away at my insides. There is no pain as bad as that. No pain.

I didn't know how I was going to stand it the second time,

and, as I told him that, he said he'd wait a minute, but he didn't, and I jumped, and then it hurt so bad it almost didn't hurt at all. Then all of a sudden, everything was wet and cool, and the doctor was crying. He had his head on my feet, and he was kissing them and crying.

"Oh, Jesus, oh, sweet Jesus, forgive me, forgive me. Oh, Jesus. Oh, don't die. Oh, Jesus, Jesus." That's all he said, over and over. The drape on me was sopping and red, and the pain was beyond pain. Nobody had to tell me I was bleeding to death.

Later, I found out that when I jumped, the instruments had punctured my uterus and gone through to my stomach, but all I knew then was that I was dying and that there was no one there to help me.

"Take me to a hospital. For God's sake, take me to a hospital." That's all I had the strength to say. He stumbled across the room, unlocked the door, wrapped me with a clean sheet and laid me, like a diapered baby, in his car.

"Oh, Jesus, save us from our sins. Oh, Jesus." All the way to the hospital he sobbed.

I awoke alone, surrounded by white. I couldn't move. I would never move again. The ache inside of me would forever paralyze me, keep me frozen in this safe, white world. I didn't want to see anyone, to speak to anyone. I wasn't angry. I wasn't anything. I just wanted to be left alone.

About noon the surgeon came in.

"What did you do to yourself, girl? The doctor who brought you said you tried to abort yourself with a crocheting hook. Is that true?"

I didn't say anything. I was drained of everything, including malice, so that story was as good as any other. He waited. Then, suspiciously, "You can tell me, you know." I knew he'd seen the blisters on my bottom.

"We have competent people who can do abortions here if you're that desperate. There's no need for a do-it-yourselfer in this day and age."

I said nothing. He seemed nice, but what was there to say?

"Oh, well, I guess you won't be worrying about that anymore. We had to take three feet of your intestines out, and whether you care or not, I'm sorry to report that you will probably never have children again." Luckily, he left just before the tears started.

"No more babies? Oh, Chuckie. Oh, Gary. Where are my children? No more babies?" My heart was crying out, painful, ready to explode. What was I doing to my life? I cried and cried then, pure, cleansing tears that came from parts of me I hadn't felt for so long. Finally I slept, a long, dreamless sleep, and woke up hungry. Despite the pain, I was beginning to feel some inkling of happiness. I was alive, wasn't I? All that blood had poured out, and still I was alive. The doctors told me that I had been in surgery all night, and the whole time it had been touch-and-go as to whether I lived.

That thought humbled me. Why hadn't I died? What force was there, what power, which had kept me on this side of the line rather than letting me slip over to the other? And why?

"I'm alive for a reason," I thought. "This isn't just luck; I've been saved for some reason."

I knew that was true. For the first time since I'd left the farm fourteen years before, I felt special, felt unique. Maybe there was a God, and it was He who had saved me. Maybe I hadn't been so bad after all. The thought was so exciting that I tucked it away inside me and only peeked at it occasionally, when I thought it was safe. Each time it gave me goose bumps.

I did a lot of thinking in the eleven days I spent in the hospital. I promised to change my life, get out of the racket I was in and do something constructive, something good. I wouldn't make God sorry for having saved me; I would make Him love me so He'd never let me go again. I was concentrating so hard on what I'd do for Him, I neglected to open myself to what He'd done for me.

I was getting stronger and stronger, eating good food and cleaning out the garbage from my system, but my soul hungered for some food, too. One day, on an impulse, I opened the Bible that was sitting by my bedside and began to read.

"There must be an answer in here somewhere," I thought. "Good people always swear by it."

I laughed at my little joke and kept on reading. It was pretty hard going, with all those "thee's" and "thou's" so I flipped ahead, but the ending was much more confusing than the beginning. It made me feel inferior and frustrated. If this book was so holy, why didn't they make it so people could understand it? For the first time since the surgery, I was irritated. God saved me, then turned His back on me. Just like a man! I buried my head in the pillow and tried to sleep.

"Hello there. Anybody home?"

A Catholic chaplain was standing over my bed. He was small and balding, and his eyes were fixed on a spot just over my head.

"Are we getting all better from our surgery? Are we going to be as good as new pretty soon?"

"Yes, Father." I could feel my pulse rising. A man of God!

"Well, well. I'm glad. I'm glad."

He looked around the room, sat on the side of my bed, said "Oh, I'm sorry," and moved to the chair sitting next to me. He kept crossing and uncrossing his legs.

"Well, young lady, how do you like the service here? Do you have all the comforts of home?" He chuckled.

"Yes, Father. Everyone's been nice to me."

"Well, they know they'd have me to contend with if they weren't. You seem like such a nice young lady." (Pause.) "Will your husband be coming to get you?"

"No, Father. We're separated."

"Oh?"

"But we're working on a reconciliation," I lied.

"Oh, I'm glad to hear that." He smiled again, a smile which looked like it had been used fifty times a day for thousands of days and was almost worn out.

"Well, you tell your young man he's a lucky son-of-a-gun. And I'm sure you'll be a good little wife from now on."

He was leaving. Did he know about the abortion?

"Father? Father, what church do you preach at? I mean, where is it? How do I get there?" I didn't want him to go away. He had to have some answers.

"Oh, my dear, I don't have a regular parish. But I'm always around. I'll come back to see you before you leave, you rest assured. You get some sleep now."

For the remaining four days that I was there I waited for him to come in, to visit me, to save me. I was weak, I was mellow, I felt I was seeking an answer, the Answer. But he didn't show up. The following Tuesday, I left.

I was too weak to live alone, and I was desperately lonely, so I moved in with a woman acquaintance who'd always been nice to me. I found out soon what a mistake that was. She turned out to be an alcoholic who, in the middle of the night, would come home and try to kill her twelve-year-old son, thinking he was some lover or another who had rejected her. She was twice my size, and I was scared to death of her violence. As soon as I could walk, I moved back into my apartment in Los Gatos, alone.

Once more, I had seen how ugly life could be. Sadly, I let that seamy view of life undo all the good of my hospital stay. Instead of seeking out the God who'd kept me alive, I turned, once again, to my own devices.

That special feeling was gone.

9
Turning Tricks

I hadn't told anyone at the Beachcomber about the whole abortion scene—I had just dropped out of sight for two weeks—so my entrance was a real smash hit.

"Judy, what happened to you?"

"Where you been, kid? We missed you. The place ain't the same without you."

"Oh," I said casually. "I just needed a little bed rest, if you know what I mean."

We all had a good laugh about how I'd put the Grim Reaper out of business, how the good die young and the bad live on and on, but I didn't tell them about the old doctor or about my strange thoughts and feelings in the hospital. It was all too personal, and besides, that was all in the past, gone. I had tried hard to conjure back that special feeling, to feel it back into existence, so hard that the whole experience wore dry and thin as yesterday's paper.

"Dreams are for babies and weaklings," I told myself. "From now on, I'm going to be strong."

Jimmy had been worried sick.

"I'm just going to have to take better care of you, baby," he said. "I can't make music without you." For a change, he wasn't joking.

"I appreciate the concern, honey, but I don't need anybody to take care of me. I'm all I've got, so I manage to take pretty good care of myself, thank you."

Inside, though, I was scared. I'd come awfully close to caring myself right out of existence. If I were going to handle things myself, I had to be more careful.

That was the dilemma: I needed to make some money to pay those hospital bills, but I needed to be careful, too. That meant no more ripping people off. I had been dealing with the almighty male ego, and it was foolish to underestimate the fury of a male scorned. It was only by divine Providence that none of those men ever found me and beat me to a pulp. Anyway, scratch that business, I thought. I considered for a minute going back to the bakery or the Brussels sprout factory, but that was a dead end if I ever saw one. I was used to making a fair amount of money now, and when I had money I thought I had power. In those days, I needed that power to feel right, to feel I was in control.

The thought of prostitution crossed my mind.

"It's only one step farther than you went before," I told myself. "You could demand even more money and not have to worry about sneaking around and getting hurt. In fact, in a way it's more honest than what you were doing." I laughed at my own joke. Prostitution was going to make an honest woman of me. I was so good at self-deception in those days.

The whole idea began to grow on me, except for one big drawback: although the doctor said I could probably never have children again, I was not going to take any chances. The memory of that abortion was still too raw, and since there was no form of birth control at that time which was completely safe, that left prostitution out. So I was at loose ends for a few weeks, just bumming around and trying to get things together.

One night the phone rang.

"Judy. Judy, don't hang up, please?" It was the old doctor.

"Well, you callin' to see if I'm still alive or to check my blisters? Yes, I'm alive and no, I'm not interested in house calls. Now goodbye." I couldn't believe he had the nerve to call.

"Wait. Wait. Judy, I need to make it up to you, to help you. Please come see me at the office, during the day. I've got something I know you'd be interested in."

"Look. I know everything you got, and I'm not interested in any of it. Haven't you done enough damage?"

"I'm sorry. I do want to help. That's all I can say," he said. His voice shook a little, and suddenly I felt sorry for him. He had been as scared as I was, and he had driven me to the hospital and gotten good care for me.

"OK, OK, what do you have to say? Make it snappy."

"All I can tell you over the phone is that it's something that should help you make a lot of money, if you're interested."

He had said the magic words. I was in his office in an hour, to hear something that would "solve" my problems.

He seemed sheepish and a little shy.

"Judy, I don't know what you do for a living, but I've got a pretty good idea. I feel I owe it to you to make your life as easy as possible after what I've done to mess it up. How would you like some birth control pills?"

My body sat still, but my mind was racing. The Pill had just come on the market, and I'd only read about it the week before, but I had my doubts. I couldn't believe anything was 100 percent safe.

"I'm interested," I said. "Tell me all you know and don't leave out any details."

He spent the next ten minutes or so talking about the Pill and how to use it, emphasizing over and over how safe it was. I tried to hold my excitement down, but the thoughts kept rushing up, tumbling over each other.

"Think of all the money you could make. Nobody could ever tell you what to do again. You could be rich. Not only survive but be rich" That was heady stuff, and it almost took my breath away. Meanwhile, my distorted mind was turning round and round like a roulette wheel gone crazy. We started talking about venereal diseases and how to look for them and prevent them, about the need for constant check-ups and a good supply of penicillin. Finally, the doctor even unlocked his medicine cabinet and showed me a junkie's paradise, bottles and jars of every kind of upper and downer anybody could want, pills to make you forget a whole world full of problems.

"They're all here, anytime you need them," he said. "Just keep coming back here as my patient and I'll take good care of you. No more nighttime visits, of course, but, maybe a little hanky-panky now and then? That would be payment enough for a dirty old man like me."

I couldn't believe my luck! As far as I was concerned then, I was getting the good end of the deal. In the space of an hour I had gotten a new profession with 100 percent safety, an unlimited supply of drugs, and complete medical care in case anything went wrong, and all I had to do was trade off, the same way I'd done with Dad. I'd seen that old doctor sick with fright, and I knew I had too much on him for him ever to lay his sadistic trip on me again. The rest wouldn't bother me.

"Shake?" he said.

"It's a deal Doc. You scratch my back, I'll scratch yours. But no brushes, please."

The cash register in my head didn't stop ringing once that whole day. In fact, I remember the drive home; it was spring, the sun had burned away the early morning fog, and my mind was full of schemes and counter-schemes which seemed so delicious. Everything was being made easy for me—the road to my own private hell was widely paved and I could foresee no obstacles. In my mind, right now, I see that girl speeding down the freeway, laughing as she races towards destruction, and the memory makes me so sad.

And Jimmy, sweet, insightful Jimmy, he told me so that night. He loved me, and the whole idea made him sad too, and upset.

"We aren't married, honey, so I've got no right to tell you

how to run your life, but don't. Don't do it. It just isn't necessary. I make good bread now, and there's plenty for both of us. What do you say?"

"Jimmy when you get to know me better, you'll know I can't take nothing from nobody. It's gotta be me and nobody else. I like you a lot, but that's just not my style."

"I love you."

I paused. He had never said that before.

"If you really mean that, you'll let me be what I have to be and do what I have to do. That's the only way we'll ever get along."

A minute ticked by. "If that's the way the lady wants it, that's the way the lady will have it. But the part about loving you still goes."

I went home that night and thought hard. I knew that when I was with Jimmy I was a different person, the kind of girl I would've been if I had stayed on the farm. I felt good and lady-like and pure, like the world hadn't touched me yet and never could. I loved that feeling, but I didn't want to let myself count on it. I felt that every time I let my guard down, someone always butted in and messed everything up. My feelings for Jimmy were too good to last, so there was no use wrapping my life around him, only to have someone grab my happiness away like Mom had done that day on the farm. Nothing was certain in life, so why not cover all my bets?

Anyway, I reasoned, what was wrong with having a few customers during the day if I could see Jimmy at night? Everyone else had something to sell. Now it was my turn to get in on the act. It was dog-eat-dog, no matter what Jimmy Mamou said, and since that's the way it was, I was going to be top dog.

All the next day I kept myself too busy to think.

"If I'm going to be a hooker, I'm going to be the best one on earth," I told a girlfriend. Somehow, working hard at the job would make it seem more "right." I shopped madly, impulsively, as if I'd already earned my huge stash of money. I made myself look as beautiful as I could, trying desperately to camouflage the ugliness I was already starting to feel inside.

That night, as I pulled up to one of San Francisco's poshest bars, my stomach was so nervous I was sure I would have to call the whole thing off, but that hard, brittle part of me pushed me in there, and soon a man with bad breath and a lot of money approached me. We ended up at a nearby motel, and although I despised every minute of it, in the same way a crooked real estate salesman has to despise the people he cons, I put on a great act, and the guy promised to see me again.

"The whole thing's gross," I thought as I pocketed the money. "I'm not sure I can take this." But I was a lot richer than I'd been half an hour ago, and already the details of the incident were getting fuzzy. I sat in my car for a while, and then went into a different bar down the street. There a man paid me handsomely for something that was almost over before it started. I just could not believe these men were such pushovers. I had convinced both of them that they were really terrific and that I couldn't wait to see them again, and they'd left scheming about what they'd do the next time to live up to their reputations. Fools. This was going to be easier than I thought.

And it was easy, at least at first. I was so busy counting my money that I didn't leave time to think or feel anything real. Just turn those feelings off, turn those men on, and laugh all the way to the bank. Whenever my conscience hurt me (which was a lot, at first) I started counting my money. Or, when I started feeling really bad, I blamed the men.

"I'm just providing a service," I told myself. "If they want to pay to use my body, that's their problem. If it weren't me, it'd be someone else." It also helped the first time I heard one of my customers referred to as a "trick."

"That's true," I thought. "He's a fool, I'm playing a trick on him, and, in turn, he pays me." This dehumanized my customers. They were fools, idiots, tricks. They were only objects of scorn.

I realize now that I was heaping the same scorn on them I had felt so long ago for my Dad, but this time I thought I was the victor. I was calling the shots and getting paid for it. I had these fools right where I wanted them; I was in control.

Of course, I couldn't or wouldn't let myself see that lying down with dogs also tainted me. I wouldn't admit that all this was taking any toll on me, or even changing me in any way. Yet more and more I avoided myself, more and more I stayed out later and later, more and more I drowned out any voice inside me which dared to question my actions.

Anyone who prostitutes herself begins to live on the outskirts of propriety, and I was no different. After about five months of turning tricks in the various bars in Santa Cruz, I found myself spending the night courtesy of the Santa Cruz jail.

"We're booking you for vagrancy," said the arresting officer. "We can't pin anything else on you, so that'll have to stick."

Jail! I was sick as they fingerprinted me, nauseous as they took my clothes and searched me. Suddenly, polite society was everyone else, and I was behind bars! In a way, I hoped they would throw me in solitary and let me stew a lot, give me time to think.

Instead, I was shoved into a cell with six other hookers, most of whom had just come from a bordello in Nevada. They spent the night embarrassing the cops with their language, and by the time the second night rolled around, my mouth was as foul as theirs. Now that they were in there with me, it seemed more like a slumber party than a criminal offense. The outside society—they were the ones who were wrong by outlawing prostitution. Anyone knew that once something was outlawed people wanted it all the more. Why not just admit that prostitution was here to stay?

They ranted on and on about prostitution being a "victimless" crime, and, for the first time, I began to see my profession as a respectable one. I felt the safety in numbers, the strength of the group support, and I was fooled by this.

In jail I also learned something I considered invaluable: prostitution in Nevada was legal. It didn't pay as much, but there were no hassles with the cops, either. I stored that away as useful information for another day.

Meanwhile, there was today to get through, and since we all hated men, we played a kind of "Can you top this?" game featuring the dumb tricks we'd met.

"Wow, I haven't laughed so hard since I ripped off that first guy at the Beachcomber," I said, and I told them that story in full detail. They laughed so hard and I felt so good.

"Hey, this life ain't bad," I thought. "Free room and board and plenty of good company. What more could a fine upstanding citizen want?" But after a day or two, I got restless. When was I going to get out? My window overlooked the Bay and each night, I saw the glistening lights and heard the beat of the rock music, the laughter of all the free people. Where were Jimmy and all my friends? The thought of them doing all the things I'd taken so much for granted made my heart feel too heavy for my chest.

"I know that Jimmy Mamou. He's probably making up for lost time with all the chicks, glad to be rid of me for awhile," I told the girls. The more I thought of it, the more convinced I became. Jimmy didn't love me. The world had forgotten me. As the long days crawled by, I felt more and more insignificant.

Finally I got Jimmy by phone. "I don't care how you do it, just get me outa here!"

"Baby, oh baby, I'm trying, but your bail is set really high. Everybody's bummed out, but me and the guys, we figured out a way to raise the dough. Don't worry; tomorrow night we'll be together again. I promise."

Three more days passed. No word. I started playing silly games with my head and pictured myself tottering out at age 65, jitterbugging at the Beachcomber with a cane, but in the middle of the night those scenes weren't so funny. I spent my second Friday night in jail looking out over the Bay, a world away from everyone I loved.

That night, for the first time in a long time, I cried myself to sleep. What was I doing here? How had I landed in jail? And Chuckie and Gary—what would they think if they knew I was here? At the thought of them, the tears and the guilt, just overpowered me. Chuckie, still living in Oklahoma. Gary living with Mrs. Moody. Why wasn't I with them where I belonged? But as bad as I felt and as hard as I cried, I wouldn't allow myself to say, "OK, you made a mistake. Now start over." Somehow, it seemed too late for that.

Finally, ten days after I had been picked up, a cop came to open my cell.

"All right, sister, beat it. Not just outa jail, but outa the city. That boyfriend of yours sprung you. I dunno how he did it, but he did. But take my advice, huh? Stay away from that musician crowd. Go back to Mommy and Daddy and start over."

It was on the tip of my tongue to tell him what he could do with his free advice, but I was too anxious just to get out of there. I practically ran to the waiting room, and I couldn't believe the Jimmy who met me there. He was thinner, unshaven, gaunt. He had been in a prison of his own.

We hugged and cried and hugged some more. Later on, I found out that he had been like a man obsessed that whole week, doing nothing but working on schemes to get me out. Finally, he and the band had agreed to hock all their instruments and sound equipment to raise the money.

"Don't do it, kid," his boss had said. "She's just a tramp. You don't need aggravation like that."

"She's a lady, man, a real lady, and you owe both me and her an apology."

When I heard all this, I cried. I had never believed he loved me so much. Talk about a pedestal! Even when I didn't deserve it, Jimmy had always treated me as if I did.

I spent my first night of freedom with him, and it was unlike any experience I'd ever had. He was kind and gentle, and I was almost beginning to believe in those happily-ever-after fairy tales which had always been just out of my reach.

But the morning light dawned clear and sharp, Jimmy was off to rehearsal, and once again, I was alone. I made myself a cup of coffee and sat down to sort out my life. Once again, it was time to make a decision. Do I stay in prostitution, or do I try something else?

Although I went through the motions of thinking long

and hard, in the back of my mind there was never really any choice. I now had a criminal record, society had already frowned on me, there was no use in turning back. Instead, I turned against "them."

"They had no right to arrest me," I thought. "I'm going to make so much money, nothing like that will ever happen again. I'm going to show them who's got the power."

I knew I couldn't risk getting caught again in Santa Cruz, so I'd have to go where it was safest.

I left Jimmy a note telling him I loved him, left my car with a girlfriend, and with a heavy heart, I caught the first bus for Nevada.

10
Every
A Inch
Prostitute

The two months I spent in that whore house (for that's exactly what it was) probably changed me more than anything had up until that point, for it was there that I rubbed my face in the dirt of the world and came out smelling of it.

The house I was at had no red-flocked wallpaper, no velvet drapes or crystal chandeliers, no brass headboards. It looked like an average motel in a dinky Nevada town, and it catered to cowboys and sheepherders on their way to Las Vegas for a good time. All the girls had their own rooms, and the rooms were furnished the same—a sink, a bed, a bathroom, a dresser—real luxury. That's where we worked, and that's where we lived, but I didn't care; I was there to make money, not to relax.

As in any new job, the first day was the hardest. Mostly I was struggling with my conscience. It was one thing to turn a few tricks now and then on my own and another thing to commit myself to it full time.

"Judy, this is wrong," that little voice in me said. "You

don't believe in God, you don't believe in the Bible, but this just ain't right. These men have wives waiting at home for them. The money they give you might be money for the new washer."

"Yeah, but who ever took care of me?" I'd answer. "I never really had a father or mother. I got nobody but myself to grow old with. If I can't have love, I might as well have money."

"But there are other ways to make a living. You know that."

"I tried that. I tried doing it society's way—being a virgin, working hard, brushing my teeth and being nice. All I ever got was a kick in the back side. Well, now society can stuff it. I'm doing things my way for a change."

In order to keep my self-respect, I fell back on an old axiom of mine: to build yourself up, tear someone else down. So I told myself these men weren't human, that they were the scum of the earth for coming to me.

"They're all alike," all the girls would say to each other, and in those days, it seemed they were. It seemed as if they all thought they were God's gift, they all thought they were doing me a favor. Many of them smelled like a barnyard, and most of them could knock you over with their breath.

So I stopped arguing with myself and started working. I never worked so hard in my life, before or since. The average age of the hookers was about 35 (two of them were in their sixties). I was a fresh nineteen, and every man who walked through that door wanted me. When I saw their wallets, I unfortunately, became the girl who couldn't say "no."

Soon I was working from about six in the morning till three or four the next morning. There were some days when I literally didn't think I'd make it out of bed, but at least I didn't have time to think. Whenever I found a spare moment, I'd mentally count those coins again. It took about ten days, but finally the sound of the cash register's ringing drowned out those voices in my head.

Soon, for self-preservation, I developed a scheme where I'd talk my way through their time and swell their egos so much that they'd keep paying for more and more time.

"I've got her for the next two hours," they'd yell. "Now go away."

I heard some really wild stories during those long days, but most of them fell into a pattern after a while. The typical trick, whether rich or poor, ugly or good looking, was usually married, but he didn't like to admit it (and always said his wife wasn't understanding about sex). He was "just out for a good time and usually didn't do this sort of thing" and he always without fail, came up with a line that I grew to detest over the years! "What's a nice girl like you doing in a place like this?" Oh, did that burn me. What they were really saying is "How can a slut like you have feelings?" and ignoring the fact that they were doing the same thing and paying for it. Yet, somehow the implication was that I was wrong and they were right.

I was always tempted to answer, "I'm earning a living, buster. What's your excuse?" or "I'm taking your money, sucker," but, of course, I never did. I smiled and acted as if that was the first time I ever heard that terribly original line and weren't they clever for asking such a right-on question? And they thought they were! They laughed right along with me. Of course, all of us were wrong, and now, when I picture that scene in my mind, I caption it, "Why are these people laughing?" Today it makes me want to cry.

Some of these men, a precious few, seemed human and nice while we were talking, and I could see where, under different circumstances, I could even have felt some friendship for them, but when that old wallet came out and it was time for sex, I had to hate them all. They were simply a business arrangement, a means for me to make a living in life; they might take my body and do a few things to it, but they'd never take my spirit or my soul. Those were far, far away, out of everyone's reach.

In fact, during that whole summer, there was only one man I felt some tenderness for, and I only saw him once. He was a kid, just a seventeen-year-old kid, and although I usually made it a practice to never take customers under twenty-one (anyone younger seemed like child abuse to me, and that was the one thing I wouldn't do, no matter how much money was in it), I did agree to see him after his father begged me.

"He's just gotten out of twenty-one months in jail, Judy, and he could really use some female companionship," the old man said. That sold me; I felt I'd spent 10 years in jail, with my mother as the warden and my dad as torturer, so I knew what he was going through.

He was so scared when he arrived, and shy, and stuttering, that I spent a long time just mothering him, smoothing his hair and talking to him. We didn't mention jail as such, but he knew I could identify with a bum rap in life and with the bitterness that goes along with it.

"You're a nice lady," he said when he left. "I hope you're happy."

Those were the most human words anyone had said to me all the time I was there, and in the weeks that followed, I ran them over and over through my mind. "I am a nice lady. I am a really nice lady."

Then, later, I began to wonder. Was I nice? Who knew? And what did that word mean, anyway? I was obsessed with this thought. I had to feel nicer than the men I serviced. After all, I thought, I don't kid myself about why I'm here like they do. I don't act self-righteous before sex or sheepish after it like they do. The only act I was putting on was the fake enthusiasm. I used to convince them that yes, they were handsome, yes, they were original, yes they were my favorite. I told myself that my lies were the same lies women and men have told each other since time began. I was trying so hard to maintain my self-respect, my sense of purity, but my actions all day and all night made that almost impossible, so after a while, I gave up thinking about it altogether.

Aside from the time with the seventeen-year-old, there's only one other moment of pleasure I remember from that house, and that occurred early one morning around the breakfast table when we all took an unusual break, and ended up consoling each other about how boring our jobs were getting.

"I've been at it for fifteen years now, and baby, I'm beat," one said. "An assembly line would be better than this." (I remembered the Brussels sprouts and debated. No, the pay was better here.)

"At least you're not on your feet all day," the madam quipped.

"Yeah, but talk about backbreaking work"

As the first sunlight peeked through the spaces of the thick, shabby curtains, the talk became more serious. One by one, each girl told of her life, of what had led her to this place at this moment in time, sitting among dirty dishes at five in the morning at a run-down Nevada house, working at the world's oldest and loneliest profession.

Some of the stories were pretty sad—stories of broken homes, of child battery, of drunkenness and violence, stories of upper- and middle- class neglect, of children starving, not for food and clothing, but for love. You name it, I heard it that night. When it came to my turn all I would say was, "Hey, I just got tired of giving it away." The room cracked up.

"Let's unionize and ask for better working conditions and overtime for nights and holidays," someone yelled.

"Hey, no, I got it! Let's start a 'Be Kind to Hookers Week,' where the guys have to send us flowers and take us to lunch."

This went on and on, and if we laughed a bit too long and a bit too hard, nobody seemed to notice.

And, of course, we all said what every hooker says: that we were getting out of it as soon as we made a killing, as soon as we had enough money to go straight. Even Dollie, who'd been in it for forty years, told us that. She sat there, with her frizzy apricot hair, her smudgy mascara and her face of a thousand wrinkles, and told us that.

After that, Dollie was on my mind a lot. We all had to sit around the bar in see-through baby-doll nighties and drink with the men before we took them to their rooms, and I'd watch her there. Her with her pouchy stomach (Had she ever had kids? No one knew.) and her saggy breasts and her upper arms which had no bones, only yellowed, stretched-out skin like the skin of a stewed chicken. Most of the time she sat by herself, waiting. When she did get a customer, she would walk slowly, for the thousandth time, towards that joyless room.

Once I heard a guy say, "Why don't you pack it in, Grandma?" and later I noticed a big bruise on her arm. She got some real wierdos.

As the weeks went on, though, she began to irritate me. "She deserves whatever she gets," I thought. "Why didn't she get out while the getting was good?" I was irritated at her because I was irritated at myself, so, to stop *those* feelings, I decided to have sympathy for nothing and nobody, not even myself. The world was full of perverts and sickies, and there was nothing I could do about it except take their money and run.

Still, I was constantly shocked at the ugliness of it all. People who have been sheltered from this probably won't believe what some men asked me to do, but it's true, nevertheless: things like making love to them in coffins, and sticking them with pins. One man even asked me to take a close-up picture of a six-year-old's sex organs and show it to him. (I threw *him* out—too close to home, that one!) I tell this all now not to wallow in it but to picture the raw evil and gruesomeness of the world I was into.

Many of these men were the so-called pillars of their society, but that's not the side of them I saw. I saw them with their masks off, their inhibitions down. I saw the dirty mirrors of their souls. The barbarism of it all just scarred my mind and further deadened my soul.

One night a really rich guy came in. Later, in the room, he told me he was a famous TV producer and mentioned a few of the popular series he had produced.

"This guy must be rollin' in it," I thought. The dollar signs started flashing. I talked to him for a long time, and tried to take great interest in everything he had to say. He was what others might call a kind and sensitive man, and quite intelligent. He told me how he'd gotten started, how he struggled for so many years, how his wife worked hard to support him during all those rough times.

"Starving together really brings a couple close, you know? I loved that little lady then, and I love her now. You should see her. She only weighs about ninety pounds or so, and she's got a smile that won't quit," he said. "I'm a lucky guy. A really lucky guy."

"Then what are you doing here?" I thought. I felt like screaming it out at him.

"Men like you are the worst kind," I thought bitterly. "You seem so nice, so kind, so unselfish. You tell me how much you love your wife, and then, with her sitting there waiting for you, you make love to me. You're the worst kind of pervert there is." I absolutely hated that man, not for who he was, but for what he symbolized, but, of course, I couldn't show it, so I kept him talking.

"You know, honey, I've got more money than I can ever spend," he said, "and a cattle ranch and a big house in Malibu, but I'll tell you what my most priceless possession is. It's this," he said, and held up his ring finger. On it was one of the most gorgeous rings I'd ever seen—two perfectly-cut diamonds standing guard over the oval ruby in the center.

"My wife gave this to me when we were dirt poor, gave it to me to keep me believing in myself. She saved up for it. I don't know how she did it, but she squeezed a little money out here, a little there, scrimped and sacrificed and gave it to me when I was so down-and-out you wouldn't believe it. And I've worn it all these years as a symbol of that faith she had in me. I think I'd sell my soul for that ring."

"How touching!" I said, and I knew then exactly what it was I would do. I spent a lot of extra time with him that night, making sure he drank a lot. I even let him sleep in my room, something I'd never done since it cost me money in lost business. I rubbed his back, I sang him to sleep. I waited an hour or so to be sure, and then, slowly, with baby-gentle movements, I slipped the ring off his finger. It took a long time, but I got it. Then I made myself scarce.

"He must not've loved it that much, or he'd be missing it

by now," I rationalized the next day. "I hope his wife notices it and asks him and he has to confess. That'll serve him right." I was pretty scared, but the more time went by, the better I felt. In fact, I felt good. Really fine. I'd shown that rotten hypocrite what it felt like to be double-crossed.

"Kid," I congratulated myself that night, "you've made it. You're 100 percent hooker." And I was proud of it.

To me, then, that was high praise.

11
The Streets Of San Francisco

All the hard work and money in the world couldn't blot out one thing from my mind: I was lonely, achingly lonely for Jimmy and for Gary. After two months in that house, I was so dehumanized I knew I had to get out or lose myself there forever.

Jimmy's career was beginning to take off, and he was out of Santa Cruz and in San Francisco now. I called him and told him I was coming back, and the whooping and hollering at the other end of the line brought tears to my eyes.

"At least *he* thinks I'm a nice person," I thought.

Jimmy tells me now that it was another woman who came back to him in San Francisco. I was so happy to see him that I didn't notice anything different about me, but, then, I had already made it a habit of staying out of touch with the real Judy, whoever she was.

"Honey, I got you a present, to show you I was thinking of you," I said. In a blue velvet box was the TV producer's ring. He was flabbergasted and put it on his ring finger, like a wedding band. I smiled to myself. "He deserves it, not that other creep," I thought,

We spent a week or so together, never talking about what I'd done in Nevada, but cementing up the holes in our relationship which our being apart had caused. A little mortar here, a little sand there—soon things seemed just the same to me. I really loved that man, and after all the men I'd been with, his goodness, like the first, sweet taste of strawberries after a long winter's famine, was a constant surprise to me.

I began hanging around the clubs at night, watching him play, but I was restless. I had been around so much sexuality the past two months I was convinced every young girl in that club was after Jimmy. My view of the world was now filtered through those lurid experiences, and more and more I began to believe everyone was to be mistrusted, women and men alike.

"Jimmy, I gotta get a job before I get lazy and fat," I said after a few weeks. The band was really catching on in the Bay area, but that was his money, not mine. I needed the high that came from that money flowing in, the rush I got when I knew once again I'd swindled another sucker. Sad to say, by then I was a power junkie, and I needed my fix.

"Baby, don't go out on the street, please? Let me take care of you. I'll sing sweet songs to you at night," he said lightly. "Just stay home with me here, OK?"

"Jimmy, you know I can't stand to be the little lady sitting at home being made a fool of. I know men, and any woman who thinks her man is the exception is only kidding herself."

"You know that's not true, Judy. I've had my share of fun, but I love you, too. Don't cheapen that."

I didn't answer.

"Just promise me that you won't walk the streets, OK?"

I promised, but Jimmy was still moody all week. He was beginning to know me only too well, and really fearful of what was to come. A week or so later, a cab driver gave me the name and address of someone "who likes to hire pretty girls." That's all he would say, but it was enough for me.

"I promised Jimmy I wouldn't walk the streets," I said, "but this sounds more high-class than that. Besides, I'm better than those tacky hookers who turn a trick with just anybody." The next day found me wandering into a furniture warehouse.

"You Mr. Stanton?" I asked. I had on an I. Magnin's dress, my hair was teased into the new bouffant look, and my eyelashes were a foot long. Mr. Stanton, a balding middle-aged man with a fat cigar, was interested.

"Come back here, sweetheart, where we can talk."

He took me into his back office, a room dominated by a rolltop desk stuffed with invoices, catalogues, check stubs and carbon paper, and about twenty-five or thirty hide-a-bed couches. We sat down to talk.

"Hide-a-beds are my specialty, but I'm always interested in giving nice young girls like you a job break," he said. "I've got a heart of gold."

"I'll bet you do."

"What are your qualifications, doll? Can you type?" We both laughed.

"Honey, I can do anything you want, and do it well."

Part of that "job interview" I'm sorry to say, was a demonstration of my skills, right there in the middle of all those hide-a-beds and unpaid bills. (I have never bought a hide-a-bed since then which I haven't considered used.) I was putting on a fantastic act and watching him out of the corner of my eye.

"He's lapping this up like the dog he is," I thought.

"I like you, sweetheart, I really do," he said later, "and I've got some friends who share my taste in fine women. Connoisseurs, real connoisseurs. Wait'll they see this!" He chuckled at the thought of winning the one-manship game they seemed to have going. He scribbled something on the back of his business card and handed it to me.

"Be at this address at eight sharp tonight, all decked out like you were today. No, no wear something lavendar and lacy. Yes, you're definitely the lace and furs type. And don't be late," he yelled after me.

I didn't glance at the business card until after I was in my car and had started the engine. On it was written the name of a nationally-known politician. I smiled. "You always were good at job interviews," I told myself. I wheeled the car around and headed for the nearest library. I wanted to read up on my politician friend and see how much money he made. At last, I was in the big time.

I don't know now what I thought would be so big about the big time. Like most people, I was accustomed to thinking bigger is better. The more money I made at something, the more legitimate it seemed, so becoming a high-class call girl was one more thing to pride myself on whenever I questioned my own actions, which wasn't often anymore.

It didn't take long, though, to discover that the big time was much like the small time, only the sheets were satin and the drinks were champagne. Men smelled the same whether they had caviar on their breath or pizza. The words were longer and fancier, but they all asked for the same thing. To them, sex was the universal language; to me, it was money.

And the money was flowing in, sweet to me as a baby's kiss. At first I prided myself on the short hours and big money. All the way to a job, during a job and home from a job, my computerized mind was turning facts and figures over, click, clicking like the revolutions of a slot machine that was gushing forth one jackpot after another.

"I'm richer than Fort Knox," I laughed. Then I'd mentally go clothes shopping, through the aisles of Magnin's or Neiman Marcus, or, in my wildest dreams, Cartier's. I'd buy rings and pearls and furs and diamonds, dresses and skirts and sweaters and shoes. "One of each color," I'd say to the clerk, and breeze out of that fantasy store and into another.

I couldn't have expressed this at the time, but I think I felt that surrounding myself with fine clothes and luxurious living would make the emptiness inside me go away. The more "things" I had around me, the more full my life seemed. I was using them as security, as something to hang onto, and I couldn't get enough of them. When the emptiness was still there, I'd go buy more.

But that's not what I told myself. I told myself I had these things because I was as good as everyone else—in this country, riches means brains, ingenuity, industriousness. And I was nothing if not industrious.

Soon I started working longer hours, taking two or three jobs a night, and then some in the afternoons when Jimmy was at rehearsals. By now he knew what I was doing, but I always made it a point to be home when he got home, hoping it wouldn't seem real to him. But the money did, and I made sure he reaped the fruits of my labor.

One day, for instance, as we drove by a Cadillac dealership, I noticed him slow down our '58 Ford to get a better look. He didn't say anything, I didn't say anything, but the next day when he got home there was a brand new '62 Eldorado sitting in front of our doorstep. The dealer had been only too happy to take it out in trade.

I loved Jimmy and could show it better than I could say it; also, I was trying to buy his good will and love, trying to smother any remnants of guilt I had left by turning the spoils of my trade into gold for my man. Meanwhile, my greed kept eating away at me, feeding on itself, gorging and growing to gargantuan proportions. One day a man called and invited me to his Friday night poker game.

"Bring five or six friends, OK? There's about twenty guys here, and we're like babies—we don't like to share. And make sure they're good looking."

"How much?"

"Enough, honey. Enough."

All day I put off calling some of my girlfriends; instead I just puttered around, fixing my hair this way, then that, trying one perfume, then another.

At eight I ran the bell in the hotel suite.

"Hey, where are the others? Where do you get off, coming alone like this?"

There were about twenty men there, and they weren't happy.

"Hey, guys, I'm a hard-working girl who just wants to make an honest living. Give me a break." I already had my coat off and was making myself at home.

"Why don't you get started, honey, and we'll start calling your friends?"

I gave them the names of some friends I knew weren't home, but by the time they found that out, word of mouth had drifted back that I was okay, and soon the phoning stopped.

Two hours later, I came home with a purseful of bills. We had a Boston fern inside the front door, and I put the money under it for Jimmy.

"That's our money tree, honey. Take what you want, 'cause I struck it rich," I said. He laughed, but I didn't see him take any money. I didn't know whether to feel proud or humiliated.

My clientele grew and grew. There was one Oriental man in Oakland who wanted nothing but a back rub; I looked forward to going there because it was easy work and good money. That's how I chose my clients—the faster and less demanding, the better. I was in a business, and, like everyone else, the faster and easier the money, the better. I also began seeing famous lawyers and doctors, government officials, movie stars, and professional football players. These men were among my most steady customers; they couldn't afford the bad publicity of picking someone up off the street, so they called me, and everything was arranged in good taste between fine sheets.

The next day I would watch them on TV giving a speech or dedicating a hospital or playing ball, and I would laugh to myself and think, "If the world only knew what I know about you." I despised them because they did their dirty deeds at night and then appeared on TV in the morning, all fresh-shaven and respectable, to make the laws of the land or spec-tacular plays on the field. I think I hated these so-called hypocrites so much because I myself was one—I wanted to live like a tramp and be treated like a lady. When I couldn't have it both ways, I blamed them.

So I would laugh at them when I got my money and laugh at them when I spent it. I would get drunk and swear and weep bitter tears over I-didn't-know-what. And I'd tell myself that I was having fun, ripping off the world.

The toll that it was taking on me—that, I never saw.

12
Ceremony At City Hall

Even though I was a prostitute, Jimmy always treated me like his princess—he lit my cigarettes, he opened my car doors, he held my coat, and together we went into the business of proving that happily-ever-afters do exist.

We would lie awake all night and watch TV and then sleep till noon or one o'clock. Then up for brunch at a local coffee shop, where we shared steaming coffee, eggs, sausages, and pancakes with anybody who dropped by. We all would hash over the gossip of the day—what group was playing where, who was going with whom. Then Jimmy would go to rehearsal and I would go shopping or on a few afternoon "business calls." After dinner, it was out to more business for me and off to the Club for him. We'd meet around one or two in the morning at the coffee shop again—then home again to watch TV or to throw one of our all night parties.

Whenever that routine got boring, we would dream up something new to do.

"Hey, Judy, what do you say we fly to Vegas tonight?"

"But you've got a show tomorrow at six!"

"So, we'll grab the 4:55 plane out." And off we'd be. Those seemed like fun, wild, carefree days to us, and in some ways they were. "These are the good old days" we always said. But we desperately needed that constant excitement, the constant feeding of all our senses to even feel alive. We were jet-hopping faster than we could think, always staying one city or one plane flight ahead of our consciences.

Sometimes we'd go on one of our famous shopping sprees. A tailor-made suit for Jimmy, cashmere skirt and sweater sets for me, rings, jewelry, anything that struck our fancy. For two kids barely into their twenties, it was like having a hot fudge sundae for every meal—we couldn't get enough of it, and there were no parents or authority figures to stop us. We indulged every appetite we could think of and congratulated each other on getting away with it.

The only place we didn't get away with it was at Jimmy's parents' house. They were strict Catholics, and they had raised Jimmy accordingly. From the very beginning, they had accepted me and loved me like a daughter, but when it came to the sleeping arrangements, I was still just Jimmy's girlfriend.

"She sleeps in your room, son, and you sleep on the couch."

"Uw, Mom, get out of the Dark Ages. Please?" (He always got respectful when his Mom looked at him a certain way.)

"Stop treating me like an altar boy. That was ten years ago."

"You're never too grown up to act like one, Jimmy. God's laws are God's laws."

So Jimmy would sleep on the couch.

I would lie awake, surrounded by Jimmy's old pictures and baseball mitts, and feel like a little girl who was being punished. Here I was, having sex with fifty or sixty different men a month, and I couldn't sleep next to the man I loved in his own home. Sometimes I'd laugh about it, but the hurt and guilt were there, too.

On the way home, we'd always have the same conversation.

"I missed you last night, honey."

"Me, too. What a drag."

"Well, we just won't go there anymore. If they can't accept us for what we are, well, then, that's their problem."

"Yeah, maybe when they grow up we'll come back."

Laughter.

Pause.

"Jimmy, if they freak out at us sleeping in the same bed, what would they think if they knew what kind of life we lead?"

"Oh, honey, they're just not up with the times. Don't let them get to you."

But they did. It had been years since I'd been around people who'd stuck up for their principles or who even had any, and it touched me that they cared enough about their God and about us to make those demands. So in those days, Jimmy's parents were the only conscience I had. It was only around them that I ever questioned my morals and ever worried about a bad reputation.

And they got to Jimmy, too. After visits home I noticed he would go to Mass for a few Sundays, and come back talking about "cleaning up our act sometime." But after a few weeks, he'd go to Mass just long enough to drop a twenty in the plate and say, in effect, "Don't bug me, God, and I won't bug you." He had turned his back on seventeen years of religious training, and he was feeling the pangs. The longer we stayed together, the farther away from God he slipped.

As far as my own family was concerned, I was pushing myself further and further away from them, contenting myself with less frequent visits to Gary and only occasional phone calls to see how Chuckie was doing.

"You'd be proud of him, honey. He just started Sunday school and he looks so handsome in his new suit and his hair all slicked down."

"Thanks, Mom MaRue. You're doing a much better job than I could ever do, and I really appreciate it."

I would hang up the phone and brag to all my friends how special my sons were.

I missed them at those times, so bad that it felt like a physical pain. I could hardly stand it.

"They're better off where they are," I kept thinking. "Look at my life. I could never raise two kids in this kind of chaos." Then I'd set out to make my life even more chaotic and wild, almost to prove to myself that I'd made the right choice after all.

So I led two lives, and kept them as far apart as I could. I used to think I left the real Judy at home, became another woman for business purposes a few hours, and then picked up my real self again later, as if nothing had happened. That "other" woman saw only lying, cheating, ugliness and unfaithfulness, and she drifted through it like a lifeless zombie, trying to forget it even while she was in it. Meanwhile, the woman Judy, was succumbing little by little, to Jimmy's love and tenderness. Maybe he *was* someone who could be trusted, at least for the moment.

The months went by and stretched themselves into years. We had been together almost three years and my divorce from Tom had long been finalized when, one day, in 1964, as we were driving home from Jimmy's parents' house, our same-old-conversation started taking some new directions.

"Missed you last night, honey."

"Me, too. What a drag your parents never give up, do they?"

"You know, we can change that."

"Them change? I doubt it."

"No, Judy. I mean us change."

It took me a minute.

"You mean . . . "

"No, no. Don't say anything. Wait. Just shut up and let me stop the car." He pulled off the freeway, turned off the engine, put his arms around me and said,

"Let's do this thing right, as befits a lady. Judy, I would like your hand in marriage."

My tendency was to laugh, to let off a whoop, nudge him

in the side and say, "Cut the clowning, Jimmy," but he looked so serious I held myself back.

"You aren't serious, are you?"

"Serious enough to have cut this out." He held out a newspaper ad. "Diamonds are forever" it said.

"Pick one. Any one."

"Oh, Jimmy." He *was* serious. My throat was so choked up and constricted that I couldn't talk. I buried my head in my hands.

"You want to marry *me*?"

I've wanted that from Day One, Judy." Mascara was running down my cheeks, and he gently wiped it away.

"What are you trying to do, make an honest woman of me?"

"You are an honest woman. I don't want you to talk like that."

"No, I think this life is getting to me. Sometimes I don't know who I am anymore."

"You're just a little girl who got a bad shake in life, and I want to make it up to you, take care of you."

"I don't know, honey. I don't know."

"We'll see."

He kissed me again and started up the car, humming softly.

"I can't believe the love of this man," I thought. All the way home I was limp from too many feelings—feelings of love, unworthiness, pride, confusion, happiness. He wanted to marry *me*?

A nagging voice inside me kept warning "Better not spoil a good thing," but I was too happy to pay much attention. I was enjoying being loved, I was enjoying that pedestal, and I felt extremely lucky to have such a special man putting me up there.

Again, there was no white dress and no big hullabaloo at our wedding three days later, just a bored Justice of the Peace and the two strangers we corralled into being witnesses. None of them could've cared less that I was, on a sunny Tuesday afternoon, becoming Mrs. Jimmy Mamou.

But Jimmy cared, and I cared, too. From now on, it would be me and him against the world. From the time they piped in the wedding music until the last run-together sentence, we didn't stop giggling once. We celebrated with steak and champagne at the most expensive restaurant we could find, and an hour later, Jimmy drove to Sacramento to begin a new "gig". I went home to spend this wedding night, as I had my first, in quite unceremonious circumstances. But it was so different this time, and when Jimmy called that night we tried to explain it to each other.

"You know, honey," he said, "you may think this is corny, but if I were to die tomorrow, I could still be happy, knowing I've had in my life something really special, something most people never have. I've known real love, and the lady I love is the most precious lady God ever created."

"I feel the same, Jimmy. I have everything now, and I love you for giving it to me."

"And you trust me, too?"

"Maybe. I'm trying to. Maybe I'm starting to."

I fell asleep that night hugging my pillow and hoping that someday I'd be able to say "I do" to that question, too.

But that day was to be a long time in coming.

13
Stripping, Silicone And A Visit Home

Dollie was on my mind again, Dollie of the shriveled breasts, the baby-doll nighties and frizzy red hair. I saw her in my nightmares, sitting on the curb outside that house in Nevada, hoping to lure in at least one trick that night. Sometimes, in the early morning hours when I couldn't sleep, I thought I saw in my own mirror the beginnings of that wrinkled, hopeless face. I was only twenty-four, but in my dreams the weights on my feet were the same heavy weights Dollie carried as she walked men to her room.

"What's wrong with you?" I kept asking myself. "You got a husband, which is more than most hookers have. You've got money. You've got love. You've got the world by the tail." And I thought I believed it, so what was wrong?

What was wrong, I now see, was that even marriage to Jimmy couldn't fill that emptiness in me that had started so long ago when I had been taken from a home where I was loved to one where I was not. I was looking for someone to love me 100 percent of the time, every waking moment, to be my all-in-all, to fill me so full of love I would never hunger again. No human being could do that.

So I worked harder than ever, and was more determined than ever to keep earning my own money; there was no way I was going to let myself be financially dependent on Jimmy. Emotional dependence was bad enough—you never knew when your world would cave in. But was I going to be a hooker forever? Where was the rest of my life going to go?

Just as I was toying around with all these thoughts, wondering what to do, out of the blue, or, more accurately, out of the ceiling, came a solution I thought was from heaven.

It was the middle '60's and one day in a San Francisco nightclub, a young lady named Carol Doda was lowered from the ceiling, sitting on a piano with a topless bathing suit on. Up until that time, strippers had teased, cajoled, suggested, but they had never appeared topless. The headlines shot across the nation, and the next night there were crowds lined up around the block, waiting, almost drooling, to get in. It seemed to us on Broadway Street that the world had gone wild.

The next night the manager of Tipsy's Club, which was later to become Big Al's, made me an offer I couldn't refuse.

"Judy, how'd you like to go topless?"

"I'll do it, I'll do it" I thought.

"Time's money. What's it worth to you?" I said.

"What about $135 a week, to start?"

"You're on!" That was a respectable salary in those days.

"Why am I so lucky?" I thought. "It must be that clean living." I could hardly wait to tell Jimmy, but the closer I got to home, the more I wondered how he'd like it. His wife topless, out in public? I was right; he was pretty upset, but when I told him that if this career went well it might be a chance for me to ease out of prostitution, he broke into a big smile.

"Let's go celebrate that new job of yours, kid," he said.

I spent the whole next day getting ready—buying wigs, trying on false eyelashes, sewing my own costume (a topless Rudi Gernreich suit, with tons of silver sequins, fur and feathers). There was no question but that I had to be the best, and who knew? Maybe this *was* a way out of prostitution.

As the time approached for the ten o'clock show, I got more and more nervous. You'd think that after five years of prostitution, nothing would embarrass me, but this was different. When I put on that costume, and the whole top half of me just stuck out for a club full of strangers to see, I didn't think I could go on. I was so bare! What if everyone laughed? I peeked out into the audience and got goose bumps from what I saw. People were almost hanging from the rafters, men and women. The women seemed more excited than the men, and they all were waiting to see me.

"I billed you as Judy Keen," my boss said. "From now on, you'll need a fake name for privacy. You're going to be famous, honey. They're gonna be pawing at you before the night's over."

Me, famous? The little Oklahoma farm girl, famous? That thought really turned me on. I had never considered fame before, at least not for myself. Fame meant public acceptance, and I was all for that. Heart pounding, I strutted out on that stage like I owned it.

And I did. I could do nothing wrong. All my years of dancing at the Beachcomber stood me in good stead, and the crowd ate it up. I could barely make it back to my dressing room after the show. "More! More!" they screamed.

After that, it didn't take long for my embarrassment to fade. The public had told me I was OK; they had given me their stamp of approval, so what I was doing seemed right.

"If they're willing to pay their hard-earned bucks, I'm willing to give them a show," I said. That made it all their fault for paying; I was merely delivering the goods. I was determined to deliver them better than any stripper in the city, and I set out to make it happen, to find a gimmick. It didn't take me long. The movie *Goldfinger* had just hit the silver screen, so the idea seemed a natural. I bought a gold wig, gilded my whole body with gold paint and billed myself as "Judy Keen, the Golden Girl." It was a smash hit, and as for me, the show biz bug had bitten me.

"I've gotta get more people in here," I'd say to myself

(even though there were standing room only crowds every night), so one night between shows, I walked out onto Broadway in my gold body paint to advertise the show. I was really the center of attention and was basking in all the "glory" when a snippy female tourist hissed, "How can you do that?" "How can you look, honey?" I shot back. She had made me feel like a freak or something, and I didn't like that at all. I was just doing my job, wasn't I?

But the Golden Girl died a quick death; my skin soon got horribly infected, and, after a month of trying every remedy, I was out hunting up another gimmick.

The next one I hit on I got from Carol Doda, who was working next door and had become a good friend. In an effort to pump up business, which was already at a fever pitch, she had decided to have her breasts pumped up with silicone injections. The doctor was charging $1200 for 22 injections, but only the love of money helped me face that huge needle. It looked at least eight inches long, and he would shoot that clear liquid ooze up through the base of my breasts.

Those sessions were torturous, but I kept coming back for more. It was a weird feeling to walk away from each doctor's appointment a little more well-endowed.

Since I am only 5'3", the doctor advised me to stop when I blew up to a 40DD, and even I had to agree. Being so voluptuous was good for business, but it was hard to handle emotionally. For twenty-four years I had had one image of myself. All of a sudden I had another. It took me a while to stop feeling like a freak, and when people used to ask me what kind of act I had I told them, "I just go out on the stage and try to stand up." But the doctor also told me that more housewives than strippers were getting the injections, so that made me feel a little better.

"They're all doing what I'm doing," I thought. "I'm just being a little more open and honest about it."

But those huge breasts became a visible sign of who I was and what I was up to, and I obviously couldn't escape the feeling of being different, of being an outsider. Oh, those first few weeks were torturous in a way because, in an effort to become more noticed, I had made myself into an object of scorn. In trying to belong, I had alienated myself even more. When I walked down the street in my make-up and low-cut dresses and tourists gawked and gaped, I felt I had only one choice—to perform. So I'd pull down my top and say, "Want a better look?" I hated them, and I wanted to shock them, too.

"If they stare at me, they'll get a show," I thought. "The monkey must perform."

Of course, all that gawking and staring pushed me into even wilder escapades, and instead of easing out of prostitution, as I'd thought I would, I somehow found myself craving that sense of power even more. Even more, I needed to feel needed. Besides, I really had something to sell now, and I soon found I could command more money. I was getting in deeper and deeper.

Money. That became my real lover. It was sickening the way I could never get enough; the club was a perfect place for me to make contacts, so I would do seven shows a night, six nights a week, and then, on pure adrenalin, would turn two or three or four tricks a night after hours. I was a workaholic and refused to stop or slow down. I would allow myself no silence, no peace. One of the more dehumanizing things I did in those days was done in the ten minutes between shows. Men would pay $20 or $30 to feel my body while I sat and smoked cigarettes and talked to my friends. I couldn't even say "no" on my coffee breaks. What I must've been feeling like way underneath at those times is almost unimaginable, but to hear me talk, I was on top of the world.

"I've found my niche," I bragged. "Now I've got love, money and fame." All the soul-searching of the months before had stopped; that little girl named Judy was being pushed farther and farther away. In fact, nobody but Jimmy could even see her in me anymore. I was truly a lost soul.

One night, on a whim, I got it into my head to go back to Los Gatos again, to cruise by the old high school and check out my old friends. "Local Girl Makes Good" the headlines would read. Or, scratch that. "Local Girl Makes Bad." I laughed as I speeded down the highway. "What about 'Local Girl Strikes It Rich'?" I had been stripping for two years now, and that one was becoming true.

It was around 7:30 in the morning when I pulled into a Los Gatos which was just stirring and stretching awake. I buzzed around town for a bit. The high school was the same, maybe a little smaller than I remembered. A fast-food restaurant was being built and a big grocery chain was gently nudging at the independent grocery store on the corner. Otherwise everything else seemed the same. Dull. Quiet. I remember thinking what a drag this place was. How could I have wasted ten years here?

I waited till eight when I was sure she would be up, and then called my old friend, Colleen.

"Colleen, this is Judy. What's up? It's been five years too long, kid."

"Hey, come on over. I thought you dropped off the face of the earth." Her voice sounded really excited, and I couldn't wait to see her. I thought she'd be happy for me when she saw how successful I was. I wanted to share it all with her, just as we had in high school, and I had a surprise for her, too. I was going to invite her to spend a week in the Big City with me, all expenses paid.

"From the looks of things, she can use a break," I thought.

I pulled the El Dorado up in front of her house and checked myself out in the mirror. Every hair of my beehive in place. False eyelashes and false nails secure. Tight toreador pants tucked into expensive leather boots. "You've improved with age, honey," I told myself. "The old town isn't ready for all this."

I couldn't help smiling as I rang the bell, remembering all the things the Three Musketeers had pulled in high school, how Judy and Colleen had been closer than sisters to me, how I loved them still.

She opened the door, and I smiled even more. Good old Colleen. She was just the same. All that sweetness and kindness still shining out of her, like she was ready to bandage the wounds of the whole wide world. We hugged each other and laughed and cried.

"Haven't you grown up—or out—a little since high school?" she asked.

"Oh, this?" I said, and I told her all about the silicone, and then about the stripping and the glamour and the fun I was having. I didn't tell her about the other.

"And how are the guys?" she asked.

"The guys?" It took me a minute. "Oh, you mean Gary and Chuckie. Oh, just fine. Growing like weeds. They're visiting my folks for a while. Thought I'd get them out of the city and introduce them to some clean country air. How are your kids?"

"Great. Just great." Her eyes kept straying to my breasts, and for the first time in a long time I felt self-conscious about how I looked.

She showed me around her house, a typical California tract house with palm trees in front and flowers and a fence in the back. She told me how she'd gotten involved in a garden club and how she and her husband were taking furniture refinishing classes at night.

"Hey, you guys'll have to come up and see my place sometime. Come anytime. You'd love Jimmy. We could all have a lot of laughs."

"Oh, gee, that's nice but we usually go camping and take the kids when we go anywhere." She smiled at the memories. "But thanks for the offer. Maybe we'll take you up on that sometime."

I had planned on spending the whole day with her, but after two hours or so there seemed nothing to say, and I started getting antsy. "I don't know what's wrong with me," I said. "The older I get, the harder it is for me to sit still."

We said our goodbyes, laced with promises of return visits and letters and maybe even phone calls if anything exciting happened. It was only after I was half way home that I realized that Colleen hadn't said one word about my car or my huge diamond from Jimmy or anything like that.

"I guess it's true you can't go home again," I thought. Still, I was hurt and confused. What had gone wrong with the visit?

"Oh well, the past is past," I reassured myself. "Dead. Gone." Still, I did a lot of thinking on that trip home.

As soon as I got there, I called my boss.

"From now on I want to be billed as Tara," I told him. "No last name, no nothing. Just Tara."

"The name Judy just doesn't work anymore. She's the other woman I left five years ago in Los Gatos."

NOW PLAYING
Nude Lunch Show - 12 noon
Every Nite
At 8:30 p.m.

Exotic Miss
TARA TARA

plus
**The Queen of
Dirty Poetry**
MISS "**LIZ LYONS**"

THREE DOLLAR MINIMUM PER PERSON
Every Nite 10:30 — 12:30 — 2 a.m. in the Lounge

14
You Can Always Trust A Snake

I discovered later, much to my regret, that changing my name from Judy to Tara was much more than a simple name change. It signaled an unconscious decision I'd been making for years, and it all came into focus while I was driving home from Colleen's. I saw that day how different she and I were, how far I'd stepped outside the boundaries of propriety.

There she was, a symbol of all I'd been in high school—wholesome, trusting, gentle. Here I was, a totally different and opposite woman. I had a choice: I could strive to become that girl again, or I could go on as I had been. But at that time, I thought there was no choice. I despaired. How could I give up all that fame, that money, that control I thought I had? And for what? For whom?

So I turned my back on "Judy" completely, on that part of me that was innocent and kind and receptive to giving and taking love. Now, finally, I was completely the other woman—I was Tara. I would no longer listen to my conscience, or even permit it to speak. I was weary of all those old wars, so I simply stopped fighting them.

"You've gone too far, kid. There's no turning back," I thought. Since then I have heard and read stories of people "hardening their hearts," selling their souls to the devil, to all those forces of blackness and despair. At the time I didn't know about those things, but there was no need to: I was beginning to live them. It's not that I said to myself "Well, I think I'll shut out the light from my life." It was more subtle, for that light had been dimmed and dimming all along. I simply cut off the remaining energy supply that had kept it flickering. I simply stopped trying to be anything good.

The changes in me from that time on were anything but subtle. It was no accident, I think now, that this was the beginning of what I call the "famine years" with Chuckie. I had, up 'til then, been fairly faithful about calling weekly, but gradually those calls became monthly. Before I knew it, I was calling only on special occasions. Birthdays. Holidays. On Christmas I'd send the best toys money could buy. I thought then that these things were bringing me closer to Chuckie, but they were really my way of keeping us safely apart. I was in the process of blocking out the past, with all its failures, and that past included Chuckie. He represented Judy's life, not Tara's. If she was "dead," so was everything connected with her.

Besides, those phone calls were soul-grinding.

"Yes ma'am." "No ma'am." That's all he said. Polite. Deadly. I deserved every bit of it, but then I couldn't afford to admit that to myself. My response was a gut-level reaction—make myself scarce. I didn't, couldn't plan that out. I just did it, almost without knowing. When hurt, then run.

So, for several years, I lost close contact with my own flesh and blood, my own son—all because I couldn't stand knowing that he might be suffering as I was.

Gary we stayed close to. He was near by. But Chuckie we let slip farther and farther away.

Oh, Chuck! If I could only live it again.

As for my career, I was getting harder and more ambitious there, too. I had always been aggressive where my stripping was concerned. When I wasn't on the stage or turning tricks, I was working on my act—new costumes, new hairdos, new makeup—my mind was constantly turning over the decisions. In fact, I would go to all the other strip joints to watch the audiences. What got them most excited? When did they lose interest? How did the act build? I felt I had to keep ahead of the competition to survive.

But now my attention was riveted on more than just surviving.

"As long as society thinks I'm different, I might as well really give them a show," I thought. I had made myself look like a freak; now my actions would follow my appearance. I became obsessed with finding the perfect "gimmick," the act that would make me stand out forever. For a while I did an act where fire came out of my mouth, but that wasn't spectacular enough for me. Later, I did what I thought was the ultimate in indecency, an act with a man in which both of us were naked and simulated sexual intercourse on stage. Thinking about it now, it makes me physically ill, but then the audiences loved it. "I'll do anything for a buck," I bragged. Soon, though, even this got old. Where was my ultimate act, I wondered.

I found it one day on an afternoon TV movie. A man was fighting a snake, and as it wiggled and slithered around his body, I was so horrified I could hardly breathe. I hated snakes, but I couldn't take my eyes off them. I knew I had my gimmick.

The next day, I got all dressed up and went to a pet shop on a nearby street.

"Do you have any garden snakes?" I asked. I thought I'd start small.

"We've got a black Indigo snake. They make good pets."

"How long?"

"Five to six feet."

I shuddered. That was five to six feet too long for me. I didn't know how I was going to go through with this. I had such an aversion to snakes I couldn't even stand to see their pictures in books. But it would bring in more money.

"Let me see him," I said.

The man gently lifted the long and lazy snake out of his glass cage and held him out to me.

"Get him away" I shrieked. Everything got small and distant, and I knew I was going to black out.

"Lady, I hate to say this, but I don't think you're the snake type." I knew he was right, but when I told him who I was and why I had to have the snake, he was only too glad to help me. "This is going to be a dynamite act," he said.

We sat down to talk, and he told me everything he knew about snakes. I took notes and asked him for some books to read. Then, when I was feeling a little more calm, we tried again.

I got as far as touching the snake that day, and the fact that he wasn't slimy helped a little. That night I had terrifying nightmares—I was being bitten behind my back, I was being crushed by an anaconda, snakes were slithering under my bed. I was sick when I woke.

But the love of money and my desperation for attention found me back in the pet shop a few hours later. Within three days I had that snake at home, in a cage, and was even growing fond of him. I found myself checking up on him at odd times during the day and talking to him when no one was around.

Soon he had a companion, and then another, and each friend was a little fatter and a good deal longer. They would lie in a cage in my room while I poured over book after book on the care and feeding of snakes. They depended completely on me, and since I knew what it felt like to be helpless, I wanted to treat them right.

I know the whole idea of this repulses a lot of people, but I was at the height of my desperation, both professionally and privately. I needed to survive on both levels, and I thought those snakes were my only hope. Sad to say, besides Jimmy, they were my only real friends. That's how bad it had gotten. In fact, I could let myself trust them even when I felt I couldn't trust him.

"Tara, those things could really hurt you," everyone said.

"Yeah, but at least they're honest about it. You know a

snake might hurt you and you're ready for it; it's people who always knife you in the back when you least expect it."

I worked with those snakes by the hour, getting them used to music, to spotlights, to the way I danced and held them. I found out quickly you couldn't train a snake, but you could learn to know him well enough to predict how he would respond if handled in certain ways. I worked like a madwoman, but to me it was a labor of love.

Opening night came and the club was packed. No one could believe that a woman was going to dance with 120 pounds of snakes wrapped around her body.

The drums rolled and the spotlights came up. I slithered out, half naked, with only two boas wrapped around me for cover, and the crowd went wild. When I saw their looks of horror, their looks of hunger and excitement, I was certain I had it made. I wrapped the snakes around me even tighter. I moved one way and they another, in perfect timing to the sensuous beat of bongos. I held the top snake by his neck, high over my head, and brought him down to kiss me.

"Ooh, I can't believe it."

"Oh God, I'm going to be sick."

But no one left. There was pure pandemonium after the show. Reporters, flash bulbs, autographs, people touching me, pushing, shoving—the whole shot.

"How can you do it?" That's the one thing they'd all ask.

"Honey, I'd dance with a grizzly bear if they paid me enough." And I meant it. I was possessed by the demon Money.

For the next couple of months people were lined up around the block clamoring to get in. They couldn't get enough, and neither could I. My ego was swelling almost bigger than my bankroll, and the publicity never seemed to stop. A local radio station ran a "Name the Snake" contest, and my favorite boa got dubbed "Bella Boa." My body was insured with Lloyds of London. I was a guest on Melvin Belli's talk show, and *Playboy* magazine mentioned me in their September issue. I wasn't exactly happy in those days, but the fame (or notoriety) made me feel better than I had in a long while.

About that time, a stripper down the street who I called my best friend approached me with a favor.

"Tara, I hear you're an expert on snakes," she said.

"Yeah. I even belong to the San Francisco Herpetology Society."

"I know. I think that's neat. Well, anyway, my kid sister has to do a term paper on snakes for her senior project, and she wants me to pick your brain, you know? Find out how you trained them and stuff."

"Well, the first thing you tell her is to get it out of her head that you train snakes. You see, you can't train them . . ." I began, and she wrote down every word. The next day she was back for more of the scoop, and I told her everything I knew. I was so used to being criticized about them, and here was somebody who seemed to understand.

A few weeks later, as I was walking down Broadway, I saw her name in lights, and underneath that name were the words "Only Authentic Snake Dancer."

I stopped dead in my tracks, then whirled around and jumped into my car, crying and swearing all the way home. I tore into the house.

"Hey, hey, what's up?" Jimmy asked.

"She turned on me, she turned on me. All my life, everyone turns on me." I was sobbing and screaming at the same time, and totally out of control.

"Jimmy, I don't know how I'm going to do it, but I'm going to kill that double-crosser." She had stolen the only thing I

had—my act, my identity—and under the guise of friendship!
I cried so hard, I actually threw up, and after he'd gotten
me calmed down, Jimmy called the club owner.

"Tara. Tara, listen," the owner said. "Let's use our
heads. Let's sue her and profit from all the publicity. That way
we'll get her in court, and we'll get her in the club. She'll be
out of business in no time. She won't even know what hit her."

Spoken like a true businessman. The advice went against
my nature, but I saw it could bring in more money, and that
was very much in my nature. Despite myself, I listened.

Snakes, Snakes, Snakes
And Topless in City Hall

We did sue, and for a long time that's all anybody in
North Beach talked about. Again, the crowds flocked to see
me, and by the time my day in court came, I didn't care who
won: I'd made a mint just by the word-of-mouth. I dressed up

carefully that day, anyway. I wasn't going to let some second-rate stripper take the spotlight off me. My shortest miniskirt. My lowest-cut red sweater. My most elaborate wig. And, for good measure, I took along Bella Boa in her cage, under my arm. I was ready to face the world, and I hoped all the world was watching.

It seemed they all were—reporters, photographers, TV cameras, bystanders—but my rival had arrived first, and was in the midst of a press conference when I pulled up.

"Oh, well. Let's see who they interview after the hearing," I thought.

But for some reason they kept paying attention to her, and I remember how angry I was that she was playing it to the hilt. We all walked down the long marble halls of the courthouse, and still she was getting most of the attention. The judge came in. We rose and then sat down. It was in the middle of her testimony that I made the move I was so proud of.

Slowly, casually, I began to unbutton my cardigan sweater. I took one arm out of the sleeve, then the other. Soon the sweater was off, and as I dropped it on the floor, I nonchalantly lifted Bella out of her cage and began petting her. In

San Francisco Examiner.

✰✰✰   TUESDAY, APRIL 26, 1966

Topless Suit on Reptile Routine

A topless to-do is brewing in North Beach today.

Tara billed as the originator of the "topless snake dance," has charged in a Superior Court suit that her act is being aped by Tosha, the star of another topless nightclub.

Tara, legally known as Judith Mamou, seeks $500,000 damages from Tosha, legally known as Pat McDonald, and asks that Tosha be restrained from doing her topless dance with "snakes, lizards, gila monsters or other reptiles."

Tosha even came around to Big Al's at 316 Columbus Ave. to watch Tara's act and then had the effrontery to ask her where she might purchase a nice snake, according to the suit.

Less than a week later she opened at the Peppermint Tree at 660 Broadway, billed as "Tosha the Glow Girl and her Glow Worms."

Tara said all this questioned her creativity and artisitic position and placed her reputation as an original dancer in doubt, ridicule and even scorn.

an instant the courtroom was mobbed. The court's officers were pushing and shoving to get a look, to ask for my autograph. Bella Boa was running wild, scaring everyone out of their wits. As the word spread, all the administrative offices emptied—everyone wanted in on the act. The judge banged his gavel a few times, then said "Forget it," and came down from the bench to escort me out of his courtroom. Everyone was laughing and yelling and wisecracking, and there I was, the center of it all.

That night, film clips of the episode were all over Bay Area TV. Jimmy and I and a bunch of our crowd watched the news over and over, flicking from channel to channel. What I saw then was a woman who had come from nowhere to the height of her profession. She was the best, the most glamorous, and was getting all the attention she deserved.

What I see now, as I remember it in my mind, is a sad, pathetic creature who had to undress in public and caress a snake in order to feel half-way human.

"This is real happiness," I remember thinking. But I was having to go to greater and greater lengths to achieve it.

15
Motherhood

Hatred and a hard heart, in the end, don't play favorites. If there's enough enmity towards one group of people, chances are that enmity starts spreading to other groups, too. At least that's the way it was for me. In the end, I became hard towards everyone.

Even Jimmy.

Poor Jimmy. I had begun my descent into my own private hell, and since he was yoked with me through marriage, I began to drag him down, too. I was 27 now, and at that old age I had become convinced that nothing and nobody could be trusted. Somehow I began thinking that included my husband.

"All right, it's after three a.m. Where've you been this time?" I'd greet him each night.

"Honey, I always get home at three. I was at rehearsal."

"With whom and for what? I wasn't born yesterday, Jimmy, so don't insult my intelligence. I know what goes on in those clubs, so don't tell me you were alone."

"OK, OK, I wasn't alone. I was with the gang."

"And what about Kay? Is she one of your gang?"

"Kay's in L.A. this week."

"Oh, I'm so sorry. Guess you'll have to switch to Marilyn now."

None of this was true. Jimmy did have as many female friends as he did male friends, and musicians have always been a tightly-knit group, but Jimmy drew the line there. Because my own soul was so untrustworthy, though, I could see only untrustworthiness in everyone else. To make matters worse, I was now stripping on the same street Jimmy was playing, so everything I saw provided fuel for the fire I was sure was there.

And I insisted on fanning the flames. I'd go and sit in on his rehearsals, in the afternoon, between my shows, any time I could. Any girl who even looked cross-eyed at my husband would hear from me. Boy, would she hear from me. I'd always had a temper, and now I had a focus for that temper—all those showgirls, those people I called "tramps."

I can't describe what a scene I'd make. Jimmy would just be coming out on stage when I'd imagine I saw someone making eyes at him. I'd stand up in the middle of the crowd.

"Okay, dollface. I saw that. Get lost before I take you apart."

"S-h-h, Tara. Jimmy's just starting to play."

"I don't care if Marlon Brando is on stage. This slut needs to know that Jimmy Mamou is off limits."

And the scene would go on from there. At first it was just sort of embarrassing to everyone. I'd create a one-or two-minute scene and sit down. But jealousy is a monster that feeds on itself, and soon the action got physical as well.

I shudder now when I picture myself in those days: I actually began beating girls up. I'd haul them into the bathroom by their hair, I'd go after them with broken bottles, I'd turn over tables and chase them around the clubs. I even bought a pair of brass knuckles. I was a wild woman, a woman out of control. I simply could not help myself. I'd get so angry that after I'd spit on, or kicked at, or slapped someone around, I'd go into the bathroom and get sick, to rid myself of all that misery churning around inside me. When I got home, I'd be sick with a migraine, sick with myself and sick with remorse. And Jimmy, being Jimmy, would always forgive me.

"Oh, Jimmy, it's like I'm another person. I tell myself I won't get jealous, I won't get upset, but when I see those women making a fool of me something gets into me, and I just can't help it."

"I know, honey, I know. I don't understand what's gotten into you, but you've just got to believe I love you." So he'd bring me flowers, he'd spend whole days off with me, he'd call me from the club every night. All this would work for the time being, but as soon as I got near him and another woman, I would start all over again. My reputation got worse and worse. Soon I was the talk and the terror of Broadway.

I think I felt deep down that I was destroying myself, and in that destruction, I was going to bring the whole world along with me. At any rate, soon I began to get mad at Jimmy even when he was being nice to me. His goodness irritated me, so I picked fights with him. When that didn't work, I'd pack my suitcase and leave before he came home.

"No man's going to catch me home waiting for him," I'd say. The next morning, there Jimmy would be, at the door of the motel or on the phone to my friend's house, hunting me down, wanting me back with him. The patience of that man. The sturdiness of my suitcase. It was a toss-up which would wear out first—Jimmy or the suitcase.

"How can you stand Tara?" everyone would ask him. "She's just a rotten little tramp."

"You don't know her," he'd answer. "Inside she's a sweet little girl named Judy."

"Well, you sure deserve the Purple Heart for putting up with her."

Finally, I did something that even Jimmy couldn't take. Convinced that he was fooling around with one of the girls in the club, I made a date with his best friend and went to bed with him.

"I might as well beat him at his own act," I thought.

Of course, Jimmy found out. He was furious. I had never seen him angry before, and it scared me and made me feel ashamed.

"Doing it for money is bad enough," he screamed, "but did you have to do it for free?" He was so upset all he could do was pace and pull at his hair.

"Tara, Tara, what am I going to do with you? I don't even know you anymore."

He went on and on, yelling and screaming, and in my heart I knew he was right. But I was stubborn, and I wouldn't let him know that.

"You taught me all I know about cheating," I taunted.

"Oh, why did I say that?" I thought.

Looking back, I'm sure it's that incident, more than any other, which finally drove Jimmy to do the very thing I was accusing him of all along.

I had been with this man for five years now; I had hurt him beyond telling with my prostitution, I had almost driven him crazy with my temper and my jealousy. I had embarrassed him and left him and caused him all kinds of grief. All he had gotten for his pains was a wife who couldn't trust him even enough to support her. So, somewhere along the line, Jimmy decided what was fair for the goose was fair for the gander, and he joined the swingers of Broadway and began sleeping with one girl after another. This decision was the beginning of a down-hill spiral for him, and for us, but we didn't look at it that way then. Instead, we just bragged we had an "open" marriage, an "arrangement."

"You go your way, and I'll go mine," he said.

"Just don't let me catch you, and don't let me know about it."

But I always found out. We traveled in a small circle, and everyone knew everyone else. In entertainment circles, a girl could be your best friend during the day, but that sure didn't stop her from sleeping with your husband at night. So I had my worst fears come true—now I couldn't trust any of my girlfriends or my husband. I was completely alone. I had cut out everyone. Those walls I had started building around me so long ago had turned into a prison, and I was in solitary confinement.

By our fourth anniversary, even though we still loved each other, the fights we were having were worthy of the *Guinness Book of World Records* They were literally knock-down-drag-outs. Jimmy never laid a hand on me in anger; in fact, he rarely fought back, but I would go after him with knives, broken bottles, anything I could lay my hands on.

And I didn't argue only in private—the club, the street, a restaurant, any place was fair game. My language was so filthy even the hardened club owners on Broadway were embarrassed. Nor did I reserve my tantrums only for Jimmy or the show girls. Anybody who crossed me—club managers, waitresses, men on the street—was in real danger. Once, in one of the clubs, a famous movie star patted my behind as I walked by.

"Hey, you just handled a few hundred worth of merchandise," I said, and out of my mouth came three or four minutes' worth of the worst garbage anybody in that room had ever heard.

"Shhh! Shhh! Do you know who that is?" the manager whispered.

"I don't care if he's the President himself. He touched me and he's going to pay."

I was ready to pulverize the whole room. The club manager actually locked himself in the bathroom, he was so scared. The men at the bar shook their heads in disgust.

I don't think I knew it then, but my fury was as much terror as it was anything. I was gaining the whole world, yet losing my own soul. I knew without Jimmy's love I had nothing, was nothing, yet, beginning with Dad, I had subjected myself to so many cheating men that I refused to hope or believe my husband was any different. There was no way I could bring myself to trust him.

Mornings, after I would kick him out, he would sit on the curb in front of our house and cry. But I felt I couldn't let that get to me. He would bring me flowers and woo me in a hundred thousand ways, but I didn't let that get to me. I was so unhappy, I would rip the marriage apart before I'd trust him.

Jimmy was loving, secure, grounded. He had had a family who cared for him, he had his music, and tons of friends. I had nothing but Jimmy and my money, and I was losing Jimmy.

I was pretty hardened by then, and the harder I got, the more lonely I knew I was. I found myself thinking more and more of Chuck. He was nine now, and MaRue and Ardean kept me up with his activities. But still I wondered what he was like, what was in his boyish thoughts when he fell asleep at night. How much did he remember of me and our past? Those thoughts haunted me when I let them.

To salve my conscience about him I began seeing Gary more and more. One day I discovered, almost by accident, that he was having some trouble in school. Like any good mother, I dressed up respectably and went to check with his teachers.

"Oh, Mrs. Mamou, we weren't aware that Gary's real mother was around. Have you ever considered keeping the boy? You know, we believe it adds greatly to a child's stability if he can live with at least one of his real parents."

"Yes, I guess you're right. That's really true."

I almost got a speeding ticket on the way home, I was so excited. Maybe Gary could come to live with us. He was only seven. Maybe it wasn't too late for us to have a real family. At last, I would have someone to love again. All night I lay awake feeling all those tender feelings for my son that I hadn't allowed to surface for so many years.

But Mama Moody, the woman who had kept Gary for so long, was heartbroken when I suggested it to her. Her husband had just died, and Gary was all she had.

"You can't take him," she sobbed. "You're nothing but a filthy tramp." She had spoken the truth, and it was like a knife in the night.

"How dare she?" I thought. She'd never called me that when I'd talked to her all those times on the phone, or sent her money for Gary, or come to visit.

"People are always turning on you," I complained to

Jimmy. "I can't have my son living with a woman who tells him I'm a tramp." It didn't take me long to rationalize away her anguish; I was getting good at applying the law I'd learned so well: when you step on someone else, make yourself hard so that their pain doesn't backfire and hurt you, too.

It also didn't take me long to come up with a plan of action. About a week later, I drove up to Gary's school again to do something which only later would strike me as questionable.

"Honey, come with me. I've got permission to take you somewhere for a while."

"Where's Mommy, Judy?"

I swallowed. "She doesn't know about this. It's a surprise."

I hurried him into the car and, with only the clothes he had on his back, he came to live with me.

I was happier than I'd been in many months, all wrapped up in the joy of my son, and Jimmy and I set about trying to make a good home for him. We lived in a nicely-furnished condominium, and we quickly redid one of the rooms for Gary. I bought him a whole new wardrobe, I gave him drum lessons, I enrolled him in a new school. In the mornings I cooked him breakfast, and, if I was out on business when he came home from school, he went next door to a babysitter. I took care that he never knew what business I was in. The stripping he knew about, but not the prostitution.

But the bitterness and loneliness inside me were more difficult to hide, and as hard as Jimmy and I tried not to fight in front of him, Sundays were nearly impossible. It was on that day that we were always home together, and always it would end in terrible arguments with Gary watching.

"Don't you kill Judy," he'd yell at Jimmy.

One day a social worker came.

"I've had reports that this home isn't a fit home for your son, and I've come to talk with you about it," she said.

"Well, thanks for your honesty," I said. I was on my best behavior. "My husband and I are entertainers, so we do keep weird hours, but Gary is well taken care of, and he seems to like it here."

Just then Gary came home from school, all neat and clean. He began to munch on some cookies I'd made, and settled down to do his school work.

Soon the social worker left. "The child is obviously well-adjusted," she said.

I was trembling.

About a week later, Mama Moody came to visit when Gary was at school. She was polite and calm, and she apologized for what she'd said. I, too, was polite, but I refused to let her pain affect me.

"You just want him back, and you're groveling," I thought.

I explained to her that he was mine, I was keeping him, and the best we could work out was maybe he could visit her for a few weeks in the summer.

She left. Poor woman. There was nothing she could say.

A few nights later, as I was tucking him in, Gary, who was extremely shy and reserved, asked me his first question since I'd taken him from the schoolyard.

"When's Mommy coming to get me, Judy?"

I paused.

"Not for a while, honey. Until then, why don't you call *me* Mommy?"

He turned his head to the wall, and, as he did, a crazy thought struck me. They say parents end up treating their kids the way they themselves were treated, and I had just proven that true. I had given one of my sons away to the very people I had been given to; the other son I had stolen out of one life and thrust into another, just as I had been "stolen."

I had come full circle, down to the point of using the same words to him my mother had used to me:

"From now on, call *me* 'Mommy.'"

16
Snake
Bite

Money made my world go round. I was earning more than even I could spend, but I was so far gone I wanted more, so I began to use my stripping as a means for getting customers after hours. It was a natural; famous movie stars and other "Beautiful People" would come into the club, and, after seeing my snake dance, they would ask me out. I was always theirs, for a steep price. To me, they were beautiful only because they paid more.

Offers began to pour in. A movie producer offered to be my Sugar Daddy. He would set me up in a beach house which I could furnish however I wanted and give me an unlimited expense account to boot. My job: to be there when he wanted me. It was an offer most hookers worked all their lives hoping to get, but I turned him down. For one thing, I had Jimmy. For another thing, I didn't want to sit around and wait for any man. And, finally, he disgusted me.

"How can you say you love me when you've only been with me in the bedroom?" I thought. I prided myself on the fact that no man was my boss, that I was the only hooker I knew who didn't have a pimp. I couldn't understand why girls would pay a man half their take, only to turn around and have him beat them to keep them in line.

I saw those girls huddled up in the corner of the club, their eyes black and blue, their cheeks puffy from crying and beatings. All the stage makeup in the world couldn't hide those bruises or that misery. They were lost souls, turning tricks and then spending their pay on drugs for themselves and a man, who would always leave them brokenhearted when the money ran dry. Even today, especially today, I feel for them. I must've known several hundred hookers in my day, but never a happy hooker.

Meanwhile, I was still trying to prove I was the exception to all the rules. I was my own boss, I was doing everything my way and earning good money at it—what more could I want? So the beat went on, day after day, night after night, six shows a night, seven nights a week, month after month after month. My life, I told myself, was the ultimate in excitement. Yet the years were beginning to flatten out into a sameness. Same crowds. Same men. Same fights with Jimmy. On the surface, I had all the glamour I'd dreamed about when I was back changing diapers in Los Gatos, but inside I felt the same.

I was coming to know in those years a new kind of desperation, the kind that comes when all your goals are met and still there is that same emptiness you began with. I had dreamed of being free, independent, my own boss. Now I was. I had dreamed of having so much money I'd never have to worry again. Now I had it. I had dreamed of fame. That was mine, too, at least to some degree. But after the first high of having all these things had passed, a terrible truth was beginning to sink in: I still felt as sad and unloved and deprived as I had when I was back at home. Nothing could buy away those basic feelings. The bubbles were gone, and now the champagne was flat.

I remember reading movie magazines when Marilyn Monroe committed suicide and crying adolescent tears thinking, "All that beauty. All that money. How could she?" At last

I understood. I was no Marilyn Monroe, but I could sure identify with that emptiness. After two years, my snake act was receiving more and more acclaim, yet that ultimate, perfect happiness forever eluded me. The laughter was always in the room where I wasn't. Even in motherhood I'd been a complete bust.

"Now what?" I thought. And when there was no immediate answer, I turned tail and ran. To my work. I was in a race against something-or-another, the I-didn't-know-what. My conscience? The demons of my past? Of my present? Whatever, their soft, padded footsteps could be heard now and again, there behind me somewhere. But when I turned around . . . nothing. Just a shadow slipping into shadows.

I had always been a perfectionist, a workaholic. Everything I did had to be done right. Unlike a lot of strippers who took their jobs casually, I was always there, makeup and hair on, hours before the show. I never called in sick. I never took vacations. Every dance I danced as if it were my last. But now I was working even harder. That's probably why I wasn't really shocked when one night, while I was on stage with Bella, I felt my knees buckle and my whole body wobble and collapse, like so much Jell-O.

"What's wrong? Is she dead?"

"She's fainted! Help her."

"Watch out for that snake! Oh, God!"

I heard the voices in the audience, dimly, like a TV set turned way down in another room. They were tinged with excitement: maybe they would see something new, something more exciting, maybe even a real death. I just lay there. Somebody called an ambulance, and twenty minutes later I was in a hospital emergency room.

"Admit this woman. She's suffering from total exhaustion."

Once my head hit that pillow I slept 28 hours straight; I'd wake up for a few minutes, glance around the room, and fall back to sleep again. It felt so good to be uninvolved. No phones. No men. No nothing. But, in contrast to my hospital stay for the abortion almost ten years earlier, this time I was climbing the walls after the second day. I could be alone without thinking for only so long before I heard those footsteps again.

"I got better things to do than lie around this joint," I complained to anyone who would listen. "I'm losin' money every second I'm here."

I called my club manager to see if he could help me get discharged.

"When are you going to get out? I'm losing money on account of you!" Those were his first words. No "Hello." No "How are you feeling?" Just money, money, money.

"I gave that jerk the best years of my life, and still I'm nothing but a dollar sign," I told Jimmy. It was okay if I complained about losing money, but to hear it from him really hurt me. Was I human to no one?

That brief hospital stay wasn't as important as what came out of it. I was angry with myself: by collapsing and missing work I had lost control, lost my balance, slipped, made myself dependent upon others. That would never do. That could never happen again. So I scheduled a visit to my old doctor friend and came home with a remedy—a shopping bag full of pills. At first, I just took a few "uppers" to give me stamina, but soon the pills got to be as much a routine as brushing my teeth. I was taking pills to keep me awake, pills to put me to sleep, pills to keep me skinny, pills to give me nourishment. Every couple of months I would visit the doctor and walk away with a fresh supply. I'd empty all the vials into one great big shoe box. "Bennies," "reds," "uppers," "downers"—it didn't matter, finally, what they were for or what they would do to me. I would walk by, grab a handful, and chuck 'em down.

How I could do that to myself, I'll never know, but I did it. In fact, of all the habits I developed in my life, that one was probably the most subtle, the one that crept up on me and sunk into me almost painlessly. In fact, I was feeling no pain at all; I had a pill for any kind of discomfort that had a name. I was going to win that race, outdistance those demons, or die trying.

Meanwhile, Jimmy had found his own way to handle the increasing chaos of our lives. When things would get too tense with me, he would tune out via marijuana, dragging out his water pipe, pulling on his stereo headset, and piping music through his brain. Gary watched. As the months drifted by, he became more and more mellow, less and less responsive to my threats, my cursing, my running around. After a while, I myself was too strung out on pills to care. Our beautiful love story was losing all its firm definitions, phasing out into a fuzzy blur, and we were just sitting there, watching it go.

There was another result of my hospital stint; I decided to look for work elsewhere. After my contract ran out, I told my boss what he could do with all of his fatherly concern and signed on at the Brass Rail in Sunnyvale, on my terms. They were fantastic: a huge salary, plus 20 percent of the gross take. No other stripper I'd known had ever commanded that much money.

Jimmy got a job there, too. We were fighting even more now, horrible, brutal battles. (Actually, I would fight, and Jimmy would listen.) I thought that togetherness at work might help us, but it was more of the same at Sunnyvale. In the three years I was there, the biggest excitement occurred when I was being interviewed on TV one night, and for some reason, my snake bit me in the back. Instantly, the place was electrified.

"Oh, oh, I can't believe it! He bit her!"

"Oh, I'm going to get sick!" (This came from a woman who did a heroic job of controlling her nausea and kept right on staring.)

"Somebody call a doctor!"

"No, call a vet."

"Are they poisonous? Will she die?"

"Hey, would you knock it off and get me to a hospital?" I was the only calm one in the bunch. I knew that, except for the pain searing down through my shoulder blade into my back, I was in no real danger. The problem was that the snake had six rows of teeth which curved inward like tiny hooks. He would have to be pried off. The ambulance finally arrived, and I was loaded in—snake and all. I had to smile: we were making quite a scene, and I loved scenes. So there I was—a half-naked woman, with a snake gouging out my back, smiling and waving to photographers, feeling once again I had ripped off the foolish world. But who was the joke on?

The next night, the place was packed. People who never in their lives came to strip joints had decided they couldn't miss this one. Housewives who had begged their husbands all day came, tingling with excitement, hoping that they might see in person what they had seen on their TV screen. The cameras and reporters were there, too.

"Does this mean that the act is kaput, Tara? Are you going to destroy that snake now? How can you ever trust it again?"

"Guys, it's people I can't trust. In fact, I'd rather go to bed with a snake than with most men I can think of."

They couldn't believe that last remark, but, sad to say, it wasn't so far-fetched. Lately, when Jimmy left after our fights, I had been snuggling up with my snakes in bed. They were warm and trusted me. I took good care of them and they knew it. Besides my love for Gary and Chuck, they were the only relationship I had going.

For a few weeks after the bite, crowds kept coming, and after each show we would celebrate late into the morning. "It's a full moon and there's nothing but animals out there," we'd say. I was into astrology then, convinced that it was The Answer. But eventually the moon sank, and soon after, the enormous crowds dwindled, too. As obnoxious as they were, I was sorry to see them—and their money—go. Somehow, they seemed to take the last bits of excitement with them, for in the months to follow, nothing seemed the same again. No photographers. No excitement. No good vibes. No nothing.

"No wonder," said one of the strippers next door. "Their own wives are wearing see-throughs now, so what do men need to pay money for? Everything they want is in the movie houses or on TV." And she was right. Broadway was beginning to look more and more like Main Street, U.S.A. And vice versa.

Later, Jimmy and I talked some more about it.

"Well, babe, it's about time for you to come up with one of your world-famous gimmicks and give this place a kick in the pants. You've never failed yet."

"Yeah, guess I better start the gears grinding," I said. But I just couldn't get going on it. I had been tired a lot, lately. The pills hadn't been doing the trick. Often, I was out-and-out depressed. I looked into the mirror.

"Jimmy, what do you see when you look at me? Really, now."

"I see the little girl I met eleven years ago, completely unchanged; what do you see?"

"No, no, get serious."

"What's eatin' you, honey? You worried about something?"

"No, no. Nothing really. It's okay."

That night I dreamed about Dollie. She wasn't luring men in anymore, or even trying. She was just sitting on the curb, a little smile on her face, waiting. For me?

I woke up in a sweat. I threw on some clothes and went down to the club.

"Let's set this joint on fire," I thought.

But again, I couldn't get enthused. I sat at the bar with an untouched drink, and for the first time in my life, I turned down a trick.

"Beat it, buster. I got more important things to do."

That wasn't like me. I was usually the picture of politeness to any paying customer.

"I gotta get outa here," I thought. I walked into the cold air. The blackness of the night was barely marbled by a few gray streaks when I started walking. By the time I got back, the fog was already beginning to lift. By then I thought I knew what was bugging me. My thirtieth birthday was coming up.

"I've been stripping for seven years and hooking for eleven," I thought. Even to me, those numbers seemed unreal.

At home, I made a big pot of tea and sat thinking. For the first time it dawned on me that there might come a day when men would no longer want me. My stomach tightened. "I might as well be dead then," I thought. For a moment the poverty of who I was and how I was living came blinking through. I saw the door marked "thirty years old" and behind it was a lady named Dollie.

For the first time in many years, I was moving, not drifting, towards making a conscious decision. Should I stay in or get out? I had to know. Still, there was nothing yet to get out *for*.

About six weeks before my birthday, I got the following letter in the mail.

December 7, 1969

Dear Tara,

I don't know if you will remember me.

I was in San Francisco for the first time last August, came into the club one Thursday night, and saw your performance. You and I talked off and on for a couple of hours between your shows, and after the last show you introduced me to Jimmy. When I left I sent you some flowers and a message of appreciation.

I would judge that you are (were?—you said that you were retiring) one of the best strip-exotic dancers I have ever seen. I say this as a fan for just about twenty years, from Paris to Los Angeles and many points in between. I would venture to say that you were one of the very few top dancers who could do a first-class straight act *and* a first-class exotic act.

Not one of the other performers I've met over the years has possessed the courtesy, the poise, the sweetness which you showed to me that Thursday night in August. And not only the way you treated me—the manner with which you handled that whole lineup of men at the bar: the phonies, drunks, would-be Romeos, insulting loud-mouths.

When I think of the nowhere town in Oklahoma where you came from, when I imagine the difficulties you must have experienced in moving from that to the "glamorous" world of San Francisco, when I think of the stuff a beautiful girl in your branch of show business has to put up with—I am just proud of you, that's all.

You deserve to receive such praise for being the way you are, and I hope that you always retain those fine, intangible qualities that made you so sweet that night in August.

Sincerely yours,
(name withheld)

That letter was my birthday present for the whole year. I read it over and over, racking my brain to try to remember the guy, what we had talked about, why he thought I was so "sweet." That really floored me. Inside I felt foul and sour.

But it was no use. I couldn't remember him or his flowers or the whole episode. (In fact, I could never remember the faces of any of the men I met at work, not even the ones I serviced for years.)

But finally, it didn't matter. I had what I wanted out of him, too—a reason to go on. Why should one of the top dozen exotic dancers in the world hang it up at the tender age of thirty? Once again, society's approval had temporarily salved my guilty conscience, had quieted those demons.

So it was that I came out of retirement before I ever went in. So it was that, once again, I committed myself to one more year's agony in the name of doing things "my way."

17
Death In The Family

After that, I got even more involved with my snakes. When it came time for them to shed their skins, I would soak them for hours in the tub, gently rubbing them to make them feel good. I was in the middle of this one day when my Avon lady came to the door. We spent a long time in the living room choosing the right cosmetics to go with my new costumes.

"Hey, before I leave can I use the bathroom?" she asked.

Too late, I remembered the snakes. Apparently, she had just sat down when she happened to glance into the tub. Two boas and an anaconda! All I heard was a deadening groan, then a choking scream. The last I saw of her was her bare bottom, undies down to her ankles, as she flew out the front door. Two weeks later her husband called and asked for her sample bag.

"She won't come near your house, and she's getting out of the business," he said. "Please mail the samples."

Jimmy and I had a good laugh about that one.

"You're sure not a run-of-the-mill Avon customer," he said.

He was right in ways he didn't know. I was becoming more and more different, more and more estranged from society, more and more alone. I worked even harder. I still had the fire act, where I swallowed flames while dancing with my snakes. At times the sparks would fly out of my mouth and catch my wig on fire. Here I was, with snakes biting me and wigs on fire and so stoned on pills and marijuana that I could hardly stand, but I told myself I didn't care. What else was there?

Even the money was becoming less meaningful. Jimmy and I had invested in some apartment buildings and a condominium, and we had a fortune in jewelry and cars and furs. My financial survival seemed assured, but was *I* going to make it?

Peggy Lee's song "Is That All There Is?" was popular about then, and that question became a part of me—it moved in and took up residence in my head, and, like a pesky tenant, refused to be evicted.

"Is that all there is?" "Is that all there is?" It whispered to me with the regularity of a heartbeat.

Nobody knew I was going through all this because there was no one to tell. I had no real girlfriends. The only times I talked to women was when I convinced them to turn tricks rather than dancing for minimum wages. And Jimmy—I guess Jimmy would've listened, except for the fact that we were barely speaking.

My only "comfort" was my pills and the marijuana I had begun smoking. I would get high and stay high for weeks on end. Whenever I started coming down, I'd take a couple more hits on a joint, and soon nothing could touch me. I turned everyone I knew onto the stuff, and we all stayed stoned together.

"This is *the* answer," I told everyone.

As strung out as I was, there was one incident that finally did touch me as probably nothing else could have, and, as painful as it was then, I now praise God that it happened. It began when the club owner hired a new manager.

"Mike, this is Tara," the owner said as he introduced us. "I want you to treat her right. She owns a percentage of this place, and anything she says, goes. When she says 'jump,' you'd better jump."

Of course, after that kind of introduction, he hated me, and I must confess I had no love for him either. To get his goat I made him hand-carry my snakes up to me on the stage before each act. Every night the men in the audience would howl at the spectacle—a petrified, cringing man holding writhing snakes at arm's length, hoping, again, to escape with his life.

"I'll see you rot in hell for this," he whispered after the first night. I just laughed.

One morning the phone rang. It was Cindy at the club.

"Tara, this is bad, real bad. I don't know how to tell you. I don't think I can."

"Come on, come on, cough it up."

"Oh, Tara, it's the snakes. All the snakes. Mike got them."

"Where'd he take them?" I was grabbing for my shoes.

"No, no. He killed them, Tara. They're dead. He filled their cage with bleach and suffocated them. Oh, they must've really suffered, they're so twisted and contorted. Oh, Tara, what are you going to do?"

For a tiny, year-long second, the life went out of me. It seemed as if I had to make a conscious effort to pull it back into my body.

"My babies. My babies are gone." I was moaning more than crying.

Jimmy couldn't get anything out of me.

"Chuck? Is something wrong with Chuck?"

"Oh, my babies. Why did he have to take my only friends?" That's all I could say. For the first time in my life, I was completely devastated. There would be no recovering from this. I knew it. Those snakes had been my friends, my children, my act, my identity. I hadn't realized how much I had wrapped my life around them, how much I had counted on them and loved them.

"Now there's no one," I told Jimmy. I truly felt as if I had lost my own flesh and blood.

Of course, in my old manner, I threatened to kill Mike, but the words sounded hollow, even to me. I knew no amount of vengeance would bring back those snakes. In the weeks that followed, I tried hard to look at things rationally, but it was almost impossible.

"Look, all you've lost is one of your acts," I told myself. "You're still Tara. People still pay to come and see you. You've still got everything you ever had." It was strange; I had everything, and yet I had nothing. It had always been that way, really, but the death of my snakes was the first incident that pointed it out to me clearly, how empty my life was. Even I couldn't rationalize that hurt away.

I went through the motions, trying to put together another act, but the fun was gone out of it for me. To compensate, I got even more deeply into pills and marijuana and started taking other drugs as well. I think, without admitting it to myself, I had been trying to kill myself for a long time. Silently. Unthinkingly. Just by abusing my body, pushing it to see how much it could take.

I would arrive at work so smashed that the guys in the band would make bets every night as to whether or not I'd even make it up the steps to the stage. Finally one day, I walked into the club, took one look around and started crying hysterically. No one could calm me down.

"Get her out of here. She can't work," said my boss.

A girl who billed herself as Bonnie Parker gently led me out, still sobbing.

"I don't know why I'm crying, I don't know why I'm crying," I kept saying. I had never let anyone see my cry before, and now the whole club knew. The pills had wrecked havoc with my body and I was coming apart at the seams.

Bonnie took me to her house, laid me down in her bed and sat beside me to comfort me.

"We're going to start with lots of bed rest, lots of good

food, and a thorough house cleaning," she said. She fielded all the phone calls, and when Jimmy called she told him that if he didn't mind, she'd take care of me for a week or so. I think he was relieved.

"Why is she being so nice to me?" I wondered, but I was too distraught to care much. Later that afternoon, when I had awakened from a nap, she came to the side of the bed rather timidly.

"Tara, remember I promised you a house cleaning? Well, I just took your purse and dumped all the pills down the toilet. I've been watching you for a long time, and you're killing yourself. Those pills have got to go."

Poor Bonnie. I really laid into her. I swore, I cursed, I screamed.

"Get me more. Get me more. I can't live without my pills," I yelled.

But I did. It was a long, sweaty, agonizing two weeks, filled with nausea and nightmares and uncontrollable rages and silences, but I lived. The whole experience scared me; it was only after I was off those pills that I realized how totally hooked on them I'd been. Once again, God had saved me.

"Bonnie, I don't know what to say," I wrote her in a note when I left. "I'm just not used to having a true friend like you." That was all I could think to say, but it was a start in opening myself up.

When I got home, though, after a few days' reunion with Jimmy, things seemed worse than ever. No snake act. No pills. All my escape hatches were slowly being blocked. But there was one more thing I hadn't tried, and as the weeks went on and things got no better with Jimmy, I began to consider it.

For as long as I'd been a prostitute, men had begged me to make love to their wives or girlfriends while they watched. I'd always turned them down, but no more. Now I tripled my price and got into it, but for many obvious reasons, it bothered me more than most things I had done. Still, I kept on. It was almost as if I had to do everything, try everything, before my soul would weary of the world.

Also, way in the back of my mind, I knew my options

were narrowing. I had had it with men, my snakes were gone, and that left only women.

"Someday I'll turn to women for good," I thought. "I'll find a nice young girl about fifteen or sixteen whom I can control, and I'll make her love me. That can be my comfort in my old age."

But there was to be no comfort for Tara. With the death of my snakes had come the death rattle for that other woman whose life I had lived for so long. What a blessed relief my New Life would be!

18
Paradise
Lost

Those footsteps were chasing me again, those demons, all those layers of built-up guilt I'd been pushing back for so long. I was restless. I couldn't get my mind off those snakes, off Chuck and Gary, the way they'd looked when they were babies. I couldn't eat or sleep. I began feeling it was only a matter of time until . . . what? I didn't know. I only knew things couldn't go on the way they were.

One day while I was sitting in the club waiting for my act to go on, Trudy, a dancer who had gone to Hawaii for an abortion, came in looking like a health-food ad—her eyes clear, her teeth sparkling, her tan golden brown. She looked like she had never seen a day of sin in her life, an innocent babe just out of the woods.

"Hey, Trudy, are you on something, or did Hawaii do all that for you?"

"It's that Hawaiian sun and those Hawaiian beach boys," she said, and for the next ten minutes she gave the scoop about how she'd never been happier than there. The people were friendly, she said, and the temperature warm. I looked at my pale white skin, remembered the drunks in the crowd, the hot spotlights, the nothing life.

"Hawaii, here I come!" I thought. Surely I could find happiness there. Gary was at Mrs. Moody's for the summer, and it seemed there was nothing to stop me. After the last show that night, I turned in my resignation and began packing—again.

There was only one thing: Jimmy. What was I going to do about Jimmy? I needed to get away from him, yet how could I exist apart from him? Things had gotten so bad between us, so ugly, yet we still both knew we loved each other, as strange as that sounds. We were ripping each other apart and then crying over all the bits and pieces.

"I'll just tell him it's a separate vacation," I thought, but I wasn't sure how he'd take it. He came in about four A.M., just as I was closing the suitcases.

"Where you going, honey? We haven't even fought yet and you're packing?"

"I'm going to Hawaii. Isn't that great?" And I told him about Trudy, and how tan she was, and how I needed to relax, and how it would be good for us. He listened, and then he said, "I don't want you to go, Judy."

"Oh you don't, do you?"

"Now don't get smart with me. Just be quiet and listen. I know we've had our ups and downs, but separating isn't the answer. If you leave now, I just know that'll be the end for us. I don't think we can stand a separation." For once he wasn't stoned, and the look of pain on his face seemed really genuine. I was surprised. In some ways, I guess I thought he wouldn't really care. But still, I knew I had to go.

"Jimmy, I'm going."

"Honey, when people are unhappy they always think if they just go to a different place things'll be different. But they won't. They'll be just the same over there, you'll see."

"Hey, wait a minute. Who says I'm unhappy? I've got the world by the tail, and don't you forget it." That really got me mad. Just because I wanted to get away for a few days he was making a big psychological case out of it.

"Judy, don't go. I'm your husband, and I say don't go."

"Oho! So now you're my husband. I'll bet you weren't feeling so much like my husband when you stayed out late last night. I've got my spies, so don't come on with that holy-holy husband routine."

He sighed. "Judy, I warn you. I've spent a lifetime begging you to come back. I cried on the phone to you. I've wept bitter tears many a night in this bed. But no more. I've had it, too. If you leave this time, don't plan on coming back to me."

I looked at him. This couldn't be for real. It was just a trick to get me to stay.

"I've had enough of your empty threats, Jimmy. Save the acting for the stage."

"The curtain's gone down, Judy. If you go, this is it."

This last was spoken quietly. He looked so tired, and all of a sudden, I wanted to love him, to throw my arms around him and beg him to come with me. I wanted to ask him to forgive me for all the pain I'd caused him. He was still the sweet man I'd always loved. But just as I was thinking about telling him that, he walked over and slammed my suitcase shut.

"Okay. Don't say it hasn't been fun. I will drive you to the airport, though. What's one more trip between friends?"

"Yeah, sure, this doesn't mean we still can't be friends."

All the way in the car, silence sat between us in the front seat. Had Jimmy been serious or was this a new form of bluffing? And he hadn't said he loved me. Did he still love me? He had to. I still loved him. But what if he didn't? No, that couldn't be. We'd been together too long for that.

We bought the ticket and sat down to wait for boarding. My thoughts were completely jumbled. What did all this mean? What was I doing? I knew I should change my mind, but I'd come too far for that. Besides, I did need to get away, and I couldn't go back now, not after I'd quit my job and told everyone goodbye.

It was only five minutes until boarding time when Jimmy started talking again.

"Now don't interrupt me, and don't give me any smart remarks, because if you do, I swear that I'll never tell you anything again because I won't even be speaking to you. The reason I wanted you to stay is because I think I'm sick. I think I'm going crazy. No, no, don't say anything. I know I've been doing too much dope. I know my brain is rotting away right this moment, but Judy, I've been hearing things." He paused. "Voices."

"Like who?" I asked.

"Like . . . Oh, I don't want to tell you. Like God or something. Every once in a while I'll be in the middle of a set or in my dressing room and I'll hear a voice inside my head saying, 'Leave all this, you've had enough. I've called you out of this.' Oh, honey, it's so weird. I don't know who or what it is, but it scares me to death. Oh, Judy, what am I going to do without you? What do you think's going on?"

"I think you're so smashed you don't know who or what you're hearing," I thought, but for once, I kept my sarcasm to myself.

"Jimmy, you're just overworked. Why don't you come with me? Junk all this and come with me."

He was quiet for a long time. "No, hon, we're on our own now. You're leaving to do your thing, and I have to do mine. I'm sorry I ever told you, really. It's just a weird trip I'm on. It'll pass." His voice was cold, impersonal again, and my heart despaired. What was happening to us?

We had started out with everything. Free choices. All the love in the world for each other. And here we were, a half-crazed doper and a washed-up hooker on the road to nowhere.

Suddenly I was boarding the plane, and the time had come for goodbyes.

"Oh, Jimmy, now I'm worried about you. Call me a lot, okay? In fact, I'll call you tonight."

"That's okay, babe. Don't bother. You'll be fine and so will I." He sighed. "I always thought you and I were forever,

but I guess we blew it. Now we're just two ships passing. . . ."
And with that, he left.

I cried so hard on that flight. I didn't mind the fact that I
was alone—I was used to feeling alone. But would there be
somebody to come back to? Life without Jimmy was un-
thinkable. Never, never had there been another man I'd even
come close to caring about. So why was I on this plane, flying
farther and farther away?

It wasn't until I saw my first glance of Hawaii that I
began to feel a little better. The blue water. The white sands.
The soft clouds hugging the whole sky. What a place to begin
again! As much as I was sick of my professions, I knew that as
long as there were men and clubs I'd be able to get work. Sure
enough, the cab driver gave me the name of a few clubs, I
checked into a motel, and the next night I began work in a
high-class Waikiki joint as a dancer. I was feeling better
already.

"Who needs Jimmy?" I thought. Within the first week I
had a large clientele, both in the club and after hours, and
most of them were the choicest, richest men on the island. I
thought that since Jimmy wasn't around I might as well have
some of my own fun, so I found a few boyfriends and started
sleeping with them for free. This beach bum. That bartender.
This surfer. That movie star. They were all gorgeously sun-
bronzed and suave, but after the sex was over, I absolutely
detested them. Then I only wanted to be alone, and when I
was finally alone, I only wanted to be with Jimmy.

Everything was turning to ashes without him. I hadn't
counted on missing him this much. I was used to that other
empty ache inside, the one I'd carried around like weighty
baggage all my life, but this weight was a new one. Together,
they were unbearable.

Three weeks went by. No word.

Finally I broke down and called him, a first for me.

"Hey, I thought you'd want to get out of the fog and into
some tropical sunshine. Come on over. I'm having a ball."

"I'll bet you are."

"So okay, don't come."

"No, no, I'll see what I can arrange."

"Well, don't do me any favors."

"I said I'd see what I can arrange. Maybe in a couple of weeks."

I hung up the phone screaming with excitement. I would see him in a few weeks! Ten days later I was at the airport, waiting, like a schoolgirl, for his plane to arrive.

"Now be sweet," I told myself. "Just act like you feel, and let him know you love him." He got off the plane, and I was in his arms and crying all over his shirt. Then I saw his attaché case.

"Hey, that's kind of a small suitcase. You traveling light?"

"I'm only staying for the weekend. I've still got a contract you know, and a booming career."

"Well, why don't you ship your career over here? The sunshine would do you some good."

"I'm happy where I am, thanks."

"He doesn't need me, he hasn't missed me," I thought. "I gotta be nice to him. No fights. No mouthing-off. I can't stand it if he leaves again." But it was hard, too hard, to try to relate to someone I didn't understand that well anymore. He just seemed different, like something was slightly off-kilter and I couldn't see what it was to set it straight again. At times I felt like I was with his double, or an identical twin. He looked the same, he talked the same, but where was the real Jimmy Mamou?

It was scary, and, under the circumstances, it was much easier to be sarcastic than to be open with him. Still, we had a good time that weekend, and whether or not Jimmy loved me, he was absolutely wild about Hawaii.

"Maybe he'll come back to see Hawaii, even if he doesn't care too much about me," I thought one morning as he was shaving. I wasn't used to having so little effect on him. I felt weightless, powerless. Before I knew it, it was Sunday and he was kissing me goodbye again.

"Call!" I yelled over the roar of the engines, but I knew he didn't hear me. Four more weeks went by. No word from him again. Hawaii was Paradise Lose without him to share it with. The days started to drag by. Slower. Slower. I would lie flat out on the beach in the tropical warmth and watch the sun, waiting for it to move across the sky. It never did. It just stayed there, relentless, shining. What did it care? One day was like the next. Its only job was to be there.

"There's no help from the heavens," I thought. By now I could hardly bear any of the men I saw, either at the club or in private. Just the touch of anyone made me almost nauseous. Out of sheer boredom and misery, I was drinking pretty much, and was trying, lamely, to put together some pieces in the puzzle that was my life. Such strange things had happened—the snakes, the leave-taking, Jimmy's "voices," his aloofness. I had tried so hard to control my life, and now everything was crumbling beneath me. Finally, in desperation, I decided to call Jimmy's mom, just to hear from someone who knew him.

"Mom? Haven't heard from you for awhile. What's new?"

"You haven't heard?" Her voice sounded strange, flat.

"No, what?"

"Jimmy hasn't told you? He said he would."

"No, what? Tell me." I was starting to panic.

"Janet's dead. We just buried her a few days ago. Jimmy was up for the funeral. He said you and him were in touch. He said he'd tell you."

I couldn't talk. Janet was Jimmy's cousin. I had always loved her.

Mom's voice droned on, flat, unemotional. She told me the circumstances of the unexpected death. The whole family was in a state of shock, she said. We talked some more. We hung up. I went out by the pool.

"Janet's dead. I just can't believe it. So young and so much to live for, and now she's dead." I kept running that through my mind, but it still didn't make any sense, still didn't seem real. I started to cry, but I didn't know who to cry for. Janet? She was safe, gone, out of this hellish world. Jimmy? Jimmy was dead, too. I knew it now. There was no doubt. Nothing he had ever done or said had impressed me so much as what he hadn't done. He hadn't called in an emergency. It was our family, and he hadn't called. It was over. I cried for Janet and for him and for me. I cried for all the love and warmth lost in a world that seemed so lousy and rotten.

That night, as I was walking into the club, a bunch of Jesus freaks stopped me at the door. One, a gangly male with a warm smile, took my arm and said, "Don't go in there. Jesus Christ loves you, and He wants you to give up this life and come to Him."

"When Jesus Christ starts paying my rent, then he can tell me what to do!" I said, and I shook myself free. He smiled at me. Irritated, I stalked into the club. As I went into my number, I could see them through the door. Those losers. What right did they have to smile and carry on when the world was so miserable? I couldn't get my act right until they left.

I was still bugged after the show, so I stopped by the bar, got a bottle of booze and started to my room. I planned to get obliterated that night—alone. I sat on my bed and started drinking. The booze didn't work fast enough, so I popped a few pills. Then some more. I couldn't get Janet off my mind. Where was she? Was there even a Janet left anywhere?

"Wherever she is, she's better off than I am" I thought. "Nothing could be more miserable than this." I wasn't hysterical. I wasn't just drumming up sympathy for myself. I was the most miserable I had ever been. My snakes were gone. Jimmy was gone. All I faced was more stripping, more selling my soul and more humiliation as the wrinkles crept in and the men got uglier. Why live for that? Why live at all? I thought hard, trying to think of one reason to get up the next day, but there was none. I hated the world, I despised myself. The only place left to go was out.

I looked at myself in the mirror. One false eyelash was coming off, my lipstick was a bit faded. I reached for my steam rollers.

"Might as well go in style," I thought. I got half way

through setting my hair, but I couldn't wait anymore.

"Who cares?" I thought. I had waited so long, really, to end it all, and now, finally, I would do it. The ultimate trip. Finally I would fill that void, that big emptiness in my soul which had begun that day on the farm. I reached for my bottles of pills and booze. Seconal, Scotch, Valium, Darvon, speed—I downed them all. This was no dramatic ploy, no act designed to scare someone. I meant business.

And, when I closed my eyes, waiting to die, all I could see were the leers and stares of hundreds and hundreds of men, flashing their motel keys and money at me as I danced by, grabbing at me, telling me how beautiful I was. I saw myself lying to them, stealing from them, cursing them under my breath. I saw myself sneaking out on Jimmy and then throwing fits of jealous rage when he was a minute late coming home. I saw the drunken stupors, the hangovers, the dope parties. And at my funeral, I saw my two sons' faces turned away.

It had been hell, and I was glad I was getting out.

19
Paradise Regained

I awoke not in heaven, not in hell, but in the hospital. The hotel cleaning lady had found me and called an ambulance. At the time I was furious and depressed, especially when I found out she usually didn't come in that early in the morning.

"Why couldn't she mind her own business?" I thought, but I was too tired to cuss her out. I just lay there.

"I can't live in this world, and I can't get out of it," I told myself. My last exit had been blocked off. Now there *was* no place to go. Tired and weak, I called for a cab to take me back to the hotel.

I walked into the room, shaky-legged, and sat down on the edge of the bed. No one I cared about even knew I had almost died.

"Now what?" I thought. "Now I'm really at the end of the road." The night before I had tried to end it all, to jump off the edge of a flat world, only to discover that the world was round, and that I would have to keep on running. The last road I'd taken had almost led me to oblivion. Might there be another one?

I remember so well that moment, as if the movie of my life had stopped still on that frame, capturing me there, frozen on the brink, the razor's edge of my existence. There was not a breath of anything anywhere; even my mind seemed immobile, fixed in that one crucial second.

And then it was that the Spirit of God began to move in the room. I know He was moving, for suddenly I found myself down on my knees, doing something I had never done as an adult. I, Tara, the hard and cold hooker, was submitting to a male, trusting a man to help me. I was praying.

"Okay, God," I said. "I don't know who You are or where You are or *if* You are, but if You're up there flying around somewhere, make my husband come back to me. And help me."

That was it—not the greatest prayer in the history of the world, but I praise God that it was all I needed. I am convinced that from that day forward, God Himself started working in my life. Of course, I felt nothing at the moment. No bells. No heavenly harps. Not even any goose bumps. In fact, I felt let down.

"So Jesus is a fraud, too," I thought. "Just like a man." I didn't know then that He is always faithful to His promises—that He will always come when we ask Him into our lives, but at the time which *He* knows is best for us. But then I felt nothing, so once more I packed my bags and made a reservation.

"I'm coming back to see Gary and check on some business matters," I told Jimmy when I called. Just talking to him made my heart pound.

That night I walked into the club where he was working. He said later I looked like an angel in a short white mini-skirt, tanned and slim, but when I opened my mouth and the same old garbage came out, he was totally turned off.

"How can she look like she's from heaven and talk like she's from hell?" he thought. He wanted no part of me.

I found out he'd not only been living with Lola, a girl who

looked enough like me to be my sister, he had even moved her into our house, another first for him. When he came home that night, both his things and hers were on the doorstep. I was heartsick, but he wasn't about to know it.

"Tara, what you going to do?" friends on the street would ask. They were waiting for one of my famous tirades, but for once I was all fought out.

"Lola's got my leftovers," I bragged unconvincingly. "Let the pigs wallow in the mud together."

One night, I cornered Jimmy alone at his new apartment. We talked about the mail, about how we'd file our income tax, about show business. Then about Hawaii, how beautiful it was, how lonely. By the time the evening was over, Jimmy had agreed to take me back.

"You seem different, honey, More like Judy than Tara. More like the little Judy I loved so long ago." He even got tears in his eyes, and when I saw them, I was ecstatic. "He cares. He cares a little bit, at least!" I thought. "Now don't spoil it. You've got him back, so don't blow it." I *did* have him back; I didn't realize it then, but the first part of my prayer had been answered—"Bring my husband back."

But I knew I had to get him away from there, out of the perversion of North Beach, for that's how it was starting to seem to me. Get him to Hawaii, all to myself, away from the dope and the girls. Maybe in Hawaii I could control him.

It took three months, but finally Jimmy, Gary and I were on that plane over the sparkling Pacific. I think now that God needed to move us out of San Francisco, away from our past lives, to get our attention.

"The end of the rainbow is in Hawaii," I thought. This time it would all be different. But it wasn't, at least not at first. It was more of the same—me stripping and turning tricks, Jimmy into dope and other women.

The relationship was going nowhere, and our lives were constant turmoil and tension. On top of that, Jimmy was stoned almost constantly now, and had lost his drive for everything but music and sex. You couldn't talk with him, you couldn't joke with him, nothing. He would sit by the hour, by the day, staring at candles, headset on, just mainlining that music, absorbing it through his pores, totally out of touch with this world. Poor Jimmy. Poor me. I think at that point we both wanted to change our lives, but there seemed to be no direction in which to go. We were at the point where we'd try anything, but what?

One night, as I sat at the club looking at the girls I was working with, a revelation hit me so hard it made me flinch: we were all young, all tan, all white-toothed and seductive, but we were all cursed. That very beauty that the world admires so much in women had been the undoing of each of us.

One girl named Julia had had a sex change. An operation had turned him into a her, and now she was completely lonely and confused, not knowing which identity to call her own. Another girl was a witch and wore only black. By day she stayed in her apartment, burned incense and played with black cats. Only after dark would she show her face. A couple of the other girls were, like me, victims of incest, and were corroded from the inside out by their hatred of men.

"Probably any woman in America would sell her soul to look so beautiful," I thought, but I could feel it, could smell it: the kiss of death was on us all.

"I've got to get out of here," I thought. The life that had looked so glamorous to me for so many years was now assuming its true colors. The process was like paint peeling off an old building, revealing the tired and saggy structure underneath.

"I'm taking a rest for a few weeks," I told the manager, fully intending to come back.

Jimmy couldn't believe it when I told him I'd quit. That news was the only thing in weeks that had penetrated into his consciousness, and he really began to dig my cooking and cleaning. Every once in a while I'd turn a trick or two, but I'd be back in an hour or so baking apple pies. I didn't know what was going on; I just knew I was sick to death of what had gone on.

One night Jimmy came home sweating, weak.

"Gimme a joint, Judy." He was smashed out of his skull, but he proceeded to get even more smashed.

"God's been talking to me, honey. He wants me to clean up my act."

"There is no God, Jimmy. You're just too stoned to know it."

Jimmy got sicker and sicker. He began to throw up, to get dizzy spells. Still, he stayed stoned.

At first I thought it would pass, but it didn't. A week went by. Ten days. By now, Jimmy couldn't get out of bed, much less go to work. One night a guy in his band called.

"Tara, I just found out that dope Jimmy bought last month was cut with ether and strychnine. Jerry smoked some, too, and he's sicker than a dog."

I hung up and dialed the number of my San Francisco doctor.

"Doc, you gotta come through for me now. I think Jimmy's dying." I could hardly tell him the story. Lose Jimmy? There was nothing in my life *but* Jimmy.

"Judy, there's nothing you can do but sweat it out. His life isn't in our hands anymore."

All night I lay beside him, watching. I watched his chest going up and down. I heard his moaning.

"We are all so alone in this world," I thought. "There is so much pain, and no help for it." Never had I felt so vulnerable.

Around five o'clock, as the room began to lighten, I took a long look at him. He looked more dead than alive. I couldn't put my finger on what was different, but I knew. He was slipping away, was half here and half somewhere else.

"Oh God. Oh Jimmy. Don't leave me." My heart was being crushed under the weight of it all.

"Judy, don't fight it. I'm dying. Just get me a Bible, and hurry." His voice didn't sound like his voice. I raced to the closet, to a box stuffed deep in the corner. I dumped it out. Nothing there I turned over shoe boxes, dumped out laundry baskets. Somewhere in there was a Gideon Bible we had stolen from a motel room.

"The other closet," he said.

I found it!

"Give it to me. Hurry! My spirit is leaving my body."

I handed it to him, and he read aloud.

"Whosoever calls on the name of the Lord shall be saved. Acts 2:21."

"Oh, Lord," he moaned. "Oh, thank you."

He was quiet then. Tears were in my eyes. Was he dead? I could hardly stand to look.

After a while, I saw his lips move.

"What do you want me to do?" he whispered.

I started to answer, but then I realized he wasn't talking to me. I looked hard. He smiled a little. Then it seemed he was asleep. He slept for a long time, and I kept peeking in on him. I counted the hours. The longer he lasted, the better it was, the doctor had said.

About ten hours later he woke up and asked for some water. Then, back to sleep again. A day passed. He would wake for a few minutes, then sleep again. He looked just like a baby to me. Finally, I knew he would recover.

"You're looking good Jimmy," I said one day. "Maybe you just needed that sleep." He looked at me and smiled his sweet smile.

"Judy, I'm new. I feel new inside. Do I look different?"

"Yeah, you're not stoned for a change."

"But I feel so good—like a baby out of the womb."

I didn't know what to say.

"It was weird, Jimmy."

"No, honey, our lives have been weird. That scene was the Truth."

He paused.

"Judy, I gave my life to the Lord that day. He told me He would let me live if I would promise to live for Him."

"Oh boy," I thought. "Now instead of a junkie I have a Jesus freak on my hands." But I loved him too much to make fun right then. He had come back to me, hadn't he?

"Well, Jimmy. Nothing's changed. You do your thing, I'll do mine."

And that's the way I thought it would be. I didn't want any talk about Jesus or sinning or any Sunday morning sermons. For one thing, it was dumb: only an idiot would believe that a man who had died two thousand years ago was still alive and powerful, much less a God. And besides, the whole subject irritated me, just as the Jesus freaks had irritated me outside the club the night I learned of Janet's death. People like that were always pressing, always anxious for you to see life through their own narrow looking glass. And they always acted so happy! To me, that proved their stupidity. Anybody who could be happy in this world . . .

So I did go my way, and Jimmy, being Jimmy, went his.

He changed so much, I couldn't believe my eyes. The first thing he did when he was strong enough was to throw all the dope out of the house. He also began coming home from work on time. I had tried for years to get him to do that. How could this Jesus accomplish it so easily?

Best of all, out of the same mouth which had uttered so many obscenities came only sweetness. Not namby-pamby platitudes. Just kindness. Love. Strength and power. I sat back and watched. I had to admit I was impressed.

"This is all to my good," I thought. Now I had the faithful loving husband I had begun with. Gary liked it too. Suddenly the house of havoc had turned peaceful. Still, I remember being afraid at the same time. What would he expect of me now? I started turning more tricks, but Jimmy kept right on living his strange new life. Going to work. Reading the Bible like he couldn't get enough of it. Searching for a church to join. Walking on the beach, alone with God. The worse I behaved, the more he seemed to love me. It was amazing. He was so surrounded and engulfed in the love of the Lord, nothing fazed him. I could *feel* his peace. It didn't seem dumb that he was happy—it seemed kind of neat.

A few weeks later, when I thought there was no real threat to me, I stopped turning so many tricks.

"I'm glad he's shaped up," I thought. "I knew I could get him under control in Hawaii."

Without knowing it, I softened.

It was July of 1971. One day I lay down to take a rare afternoon nap, but I couldn't sleep. Next to the bed, on our nightstand, was Jimmy's Bible. He was gone. The house was empty. On a whim, I opened it and began reading.

"I've read everything from 'Snow White' to *Playboy*," I thought. "I might as well try this."

I began to leaf through at a part called "John."

"Whatever I read, I read," I thought. The words didn't make all that much sense at first. I knew I was in the middle of some great drama, but I didn't know what it was about. The temple police were saying to the Pharisees (whoever they were) that Jesus had told them wonderful things.

"We've never heard anything like it," they said.

"He must've been a real spellbinder," I thought. "Real show biz."

I read on. There, in John 8, I found it: a section I knew had been written for me—about me. A woman had been taken in adultery.

"He's going to smash her underfoot," I thought. I was afraid to go on. Why should I be put down again?

"Where are your accusers? Didn't even one of them condemn you?" he was asking her.

"No sir," she said.

"Neither do I condemn you. Go and sin no more."

Neither do I? Go and sin no more? I read that again, and then again. Jesus didn't hate her, didn't look down on her, could forgive her? How could that be? I always thought Jesus was a judge, a big hypocritical judge, out to get me.

He cared for her, loved her?

Slowly, almost timidly, my mind grasped the full meaning of that: if He could love her, that might mean He could love me, too. If He could forgive her, He could forgive me.

And then I could feel it, the best news of all: He *already had* forgiven me! His Holy Spirit was working in my heart, moving through me, filling me with Himself, and I *knew*: I was His.

I sobbed.

I put down that Book and just sobbed. I was choking and crying and laughing, and my voice made a funny gasping sound, but I didn't care. I had found a Man who couldn't be bought. A Man who could be completely trusted. I had found the Truth, and the Truth was setting me free.

I groped halfway to the Kleenex box, turned back, grabbed the Bible and read it as I headed toward the Kleenex again.

"God is talking to me," I thought. "I know for certain that this is His Holy Book and that the God of heaven and earth is using it to talk to me." I was calmer now, beyond the chills and goose bumps, as I read and listened to Him speak to my heart. He told me then that Jesus, His Son, had been God himself in human flesh.

He had walked on this earth, working miracles, proving to me He was God.

He had been tortured and had suffered and died on a cross—for me. That part hurt. I couldn't comprehend how someone, much less God Himself, could love me that much. But there was no doubt in my mind it was true.

"Oh Jesus, what have I done for you?" was all I could ask.

Then I read that He rose from the dead, proving that He was, indeed, divine. Jesus was alive! He was *the* God, not a god. He was the only Way.

I could hardly take that all in, and then I read this passage: "I am the Light of the world. So if you follow me, you won't be stumbling through the darkness, for living light will flood your path" (John 8:12 TLB). Those were more than just words to me—they were an experience I was living at that very minute. My whole life had been a stumbling through darkness, and now the living Light was inside me, cleansing me, purifying me. I was feeling the power of that Light, of that Word. I was experiencing a miracle, the miracle of new birth. Once more I read.

"To all who received Him, He gave the right to become children of God" (see John 1:12). That was it! That was all I needed to hear. That hot day in Hawaii, crying and full of joy, once more I knelt down by my bed and said a prayer.

"Lord, I have nothing at all to give you but my life. It's yours, Lord. Take it and use it as you will."

As I arose, I was filled with His Spirit. I had died to sin and was a new creature. I stood before Him then, pure as a virgin. Tara, that other woman, was only a memory. The other half of my prayer, "Help me," had been answered, and without looking in the mirror, I knew: I was glowing from the inside out. Like Moses, my face was shining. We had both been to the mountaintop and had seen God.

When Jimmy walked in, I didn't have to say a word.

"You found Him," he said. "I knew as I walked in. I felt the presence of the Lord in my house."

And then he bent down and gave me the first real kiss I had ever had.

20
"Giving It Away For Free"

In the following weeks there was no question in my mind about what I had to do. Every time the phone rang, I would jump to get it.

"Tara, can you make it tonight?"

"Yeah, and I've got a surprise for you. I'm giving it away for free. Let's meet at my place."

They would come to the house, all eager and excited, only to be greeted at the door by Jimmy and me.

"Come on in, Johnny, we are giving it away—the Good News we've found. Please let us tell you. Please?"

At first they were disappointed, of course, but they could always see the joy on our faces and hear the excitement in our voices. Almost all came in to listen. Some came back again to hear more, others turned away.

I would watch them walk away and hurt inside. I knew where they were coming from, what kind of miserable, unhappy lives had led them to call a hooker in the first place. I wanted to say, "Hey, all that pain you're going through isn't necessary. You don't have to drink so much or pop pills or worry or be tense. There's just no need once Jesus is in your life."

And that was so true. I couldn't get over how good I was feeling—the Lord was really blessing me, and the freedom of living without that load of guilt on me made me feel newly born. That's why that expression "born again" was so right-on in my case. It was like my eyes had been closed for thirty-one years, and now they were opened; I had been blind, but now I could see.

What I saw was the futility, the hopelessness of a life without Christ. I knew there were lots of pleasures, lots of success, lots of goals to meet and challenges to conquer in the world, but now I saw something that most people don't usually see until they get old and they've already spent a lifetime chasing these things. I saw that all these things—riches, success, popularity, achievements—can only give temporary happiness if a person is not "right" (at peace) inside himself. I had begun to sense the hollowness of life before my conversion, but then I was left with only the question "What now?"

God, in His goodness, had answered that question with a gift: His Holy Spirit, who brought me a peace so profound that all that emptiness went away. I wasn't changed into a mindless, blithering Bible-spouting fanatic. I still had trouble controlling my temper at first, had problems learning to trust people. And, in the middle of the night, many of my former sexual escapades would come back to haunt me. But from the beginning, I knew that I could more than conquer them, with God's help.

In fact, from the moment of my conversion, God had been slowly changing me, refining me, from the inside out.

He did such a good job that for months and months I was soft and pliable as putty. He had broken the concrete shell around me and turned me into mush. I can't tell you what a relief that was after all those years of hardness, of "me-first," of doing things my way. Now, at last, I had Someone to depend on, Someone who would never let me down. Now I

could afford to be "soft" without worrying about the conse-
quences. I rested in His arms.

In those first few weeks I did almost nothing but read
Scripture, not out of any duty but because it was such a joy
and comfort to me. It was just pure delight to discover the
blessings that were awaiting us in our new life. Jimmy and I
would sit on the couch by the hour, totally happy, each
reading our Bibles and interrupting each other and laughing
and hugging and reading some more. Gary would watch us in
amazement.

"Oh, wow!" I'd hear Jimmy whisper over and over again.

Or he'd say, "Hey, Judy! God chose us from the very
beginning! Turn to Romans 8:30.

"And having chosen us, he called us to come to him; and
when we came, he declared us 'not guilty,' filled us with
Christ's goodness, gave us right standing with himself, and
promised us his glory" (TLB).

"Hon, I know that's true. Despite all the things I've
done, I feel now, know now, that I'm filled with Christ's
goodness. That's so neat!"

"Yeah, honey, but read on, it gets better: 'What can we
ever say to such wonderful things as these? If God is on our
side, who can ever be against us?'" (v. 31 TLB). "Hey,
Judy—you know that means that all those battles you fought
in your head against my so-called girlfriends, against the men
you hated, even against your Dad—do you realize now that all
that is a thing of the past? Those people, those circumstances
can never really touch you again if you stay close to Him."

That, too, was true; there was no doubt in my mind. The
Holy Spirit was ministering to me, healing me of all the
memories, the wrongs that had been done to me and by me.

Jimmy continued reading. "Since he did not spare even
his own Son for us but gave him up for us all, won't he also
surely give us everything else?" (v. 32 TLB). That passage
really hit me. All my striving for worldly goods had been
pointless. God was our Source—all would come from Him.

Who dares accuse us whom God has chosen for his own?
Will God? No! He is the one who has forgiven us and given us

right standing with himself. Who then will condemn us? Will Christ? *No!* For he is the one who died for us and came back to life again for us and is sitting at the place of highest honor next to God, pleading for us there in heaven" (vv. 33, 34 TLB).

At that point, or whenever I heard or read again that no one could condemn me, that God Himself had forgiven me, I would always start crying with joy and relief. I cried constantly in those months, tears which should've been cried years earlier. Now the love of Jesus had turned them into tears of joy.

I don't think anyone will ever know how much that simple message of salvation means to me. I am whole. I am free. I am a child of God, my bounteous Father, and Romans 8 told me to hold my head high and praise Him for what He had done for me.

"And so we should not be like cringing, fearful slaves, but we should behave like God's very own children, adopted into the bosom of his family, and calling to him 'Father, Father' " (v. 15 TLB). That passage almost wiped me out with joy—me, the little girl who never had a family she felt loved by, who had never had a father she could trust—now I had both. The family of all of God's children everywhere, the love of a heavenly Father who promised He would never leave me or forsake me.

As we drank in the living water from His Word, it seemed to us His blessings never ended. They were most apparent then in our marriage. We talked differently, we felt differently, we loved differently.

"It's so strange, Jimmy. Instead of asking 'What's Jimmy done for me lately?' all I want to ask is, 'What can I do for Jimmy?' I never thought I'd feel that way."

"That alone is enough to make me believe in miracles," he said. But he knew what I meant. He was feeling the same way about me. We prayed a lot that God would bless our marriage, and the answer to those prayers was anything but subtle. Each day we drew closer. We had no taste for all-night parties now, or pills or dope or booze. Submission to God's laws was giving us freedom—the ultimate freedom of living with true joy. So all our excitement was in the Lord and what He was doing in our lives.

We walked on the beach. We sang. We prayed together and grew together. God even blessed us where I had done most of my sinning—in our sex life. Before, I had always thought I'd known what real love and lovemaking were, but after Jesus became Lord and Master of our home, He led our relationship into incredible depths.

Our old friends kept dropping by, but gradually, when they found out that although we still loved them, they couldn't smoke dope or have sex in our house, they left. We kept communication open with them, but meanwhile we were finding all sorts of new friends in the church we had joined. Again, we were shocked. They were real friends, not the kind we'd had before. The difference: they cared about us as much as they cared about themselves. Meeting them made my head spin. I remember one day especially: I had been feeling ill, strange, and I was wondering what was going on. I told one of my new friends.

"Let's pray about it," she said.

"Here? Now?" It was 8:30 on a Saturday evening, and a bunch of us were sitting on the porch, the smell of barbecued ribs fresh in the air.

"Yeah, here and now," Carole said. "What's so weird about that?"

"I guess I'm surprised that you want to pray for me."

She looked at me, and I saw the gentleness on her face. Before I could stop them, tears filled my eyes. I was used to Jimmy's love, but not anyone else's.

Experiences like that kept happening and happening. I made a special point of seeking out some of Jimmy's old girlfriends. I wanted them to see how much I was changing, to feel what I was feeling. When I saw them, I knew the power in me was real: only six weeks before I had been spitting on them, cursing them and beating them up. Now I felt only love for them.

They could feel that love, and they said they could see

changes in me. My voice was gentler. My language was purer. My face was softer. I couldn't see these things myself, but it pleased me to know that the Light shining in me was also shining out into the world.

"Tara, what's gotten into you?" they'd say, and then I'd have a chance to share a little with them, to tell them that I no longer stayed awake nights plotting revenge on my "enemies" because I knew God loved them and had created them. That made them, and everyone, lovable to me.

I also told them that I had read Psalm 19:14: "Let the words of my mouth and the meditation of my heart be acceptable in thy sight, O Lord," (KJV) so I knew I could no longer use four-letter words—and I had no desire to.

"Why can't you be a Christian and a stripper, too?" one former customer asked me.

"Well, I've been reading my Bible, and I just don't find any great demand for strippers in heaven," was my answer. In fact, all thoughts of prostitution, adultery and sexual suggestiveness were almost repulsive to me now. It's not that I thought, "Oh, oh! I want to do those things, but I have to act like a Christian, so I'd better not." I just didn't want to. The Bible says that sin is fun for a season, and I had long outlived that season.

Even the way I dressed was different. I started feeling so warm and clean and good inside that outward trappings such as jewelry and wigs and expensive furs just seemed redundant. They just hung and hung in my closet. After a while, I sold them.

One other thing changed: my name. I asked everyone to call me Judy. Tara was dead at last.

That long and lazy Hawaiian summer was a special one in our lives, and every day was filled with new discoveries, but the high point, I think, came one Sunday morning when we woke up at four A.M. and went down to a strip joint where I used to work. It was just closing, and we had promised Sherry, a girl I had worked with, that she could be with us on this most special of mornings. She climbed in the car, and we sped towards the beach. We had read about Jesus and His baptism as an adult, and we wanted that, too. So we'd consulted our minister.

"Why not be baptised in front of the whole congregation?" he had suggested.

"No, I can't. I'd feel like I was on stage again, and I'm not ready for that," I said. I had no desire to be the center of attention. So it was just Jimmy, me, Gary, the pastor, and Sherry (false eyelashes and all) that early Sunday morning—five of us, the blue-gray Pacific, and the Lord of heaven and earth.

"Now I have everything," I thought as I was being baptised. "A real Father, who loves me with no strings attached; His Son, who loved me enough to offer His life for me; and His Spirit, who gives me power and peace." What a sweet and holy moment that was. Never in my whole life had I felt so at peace.

21 True Confessions

The end of that summer rolled over us unawares, and with it came the question of what to do with our lives, how to earn a living now that my income was gone. We had no desire any more for great wealth—we were rich in the lord. We just wondered how best to serve Him.

We prayed about it.

"Lord, I've only got my music, but music takes me into a past life I want to forget," Jimmy prayed. "Show me what to do. Give me the strength to seek new work, if that's what You want."

So Jimmy gave up his beloved music and went looking for straight work—shoe salesman, grocery box boy, taxi driver. All those doors were closed. One day an offer came over the phone.

"Jimmy, how'd you like to work in a dinner club? The clientele is respectable and the atmosphere is tasteful."

"Great, if I can choose my own music."

"You name it."

Jimmy rehearsed his act all day, and started that night singing secular tunes with the religious lyrics he had composed. The audiences loved him, and they listened to his message. When they cried in their beers he gave them free Bibles and said, "This has the answer to your problems."

Meanwhile, I was content to stay at home with Gary and let Jimmy earn the living, but as the months went by, I felt more and more that God was calling me to serve Him more directly. I was confused because I felt I had no talent to use for Him. It didn't take a college education to realize that stripping for Jesus just wouldn't quite make it.

"Lord, use me as You will," I prayed, and I rested in that.

One day, about six months after my conversion, as I was sitting in church the pastor asked me if I'd like to share my testimony.

"Me?" I gulped. How did I get up in front of a bunch of lifelong Christians and say, "For the last thirteen years I spent all my time seducing men?" No way! But I did manage to say, "Well, I was an entertainer who lived very much in the world and found no happiness until I met the Lord," or something like that. And then I sat down, or rather slumped down, into my seat. After the service a few people asked me if I could share the same testimony at the Hilton Hawaiian at a Jesus Birthday Party.

"Sure," I said, and then ran home in a panic. But that panic was nothing compared to the fear I felt when I arrived at the party a few weeks later. There were at least 600 people at the gathering, and more were pouring in all the time.

"I can't do this," I told a man backstage.

"We can do all things through Christ, who strengthens us," he said with a kind smile, and it was that verse (Philippians 4:13) which got me through the ten-minute testimony. Again, I said I had been an "entertainer" and I also told a little bit about the drugs I'd been into. I also said I'd found out the hard way that God's laws are meant to protect us from all the pain of the world, not to deprive us of its pleasures.

"Thank goodness that's over," I whispered to Jimmy as I sat down. I felt in those days that anyone who had been a

Christian all his life was the next thing to an angel, and I was the black sheep people could barely tolerate. I had no "right" to tell them anything!

But apparently they thought otherwise. When I got home, the phone was ringing off the hook.

"When can we hear more of your testimony?" they all wanted to know.

"The Lord really knows what He's doing," said Jimmy. "All that training you've had in front of audiences is now working for Him." But there was still the dilemma of what to tell, so Jimmy and I set about carefully looking at the past to see if we could make some sense out of all those lost and lonely years.

"I couldn't see it then, but I can see it now, how the Lord was guiding me all the time," I told Jimmy. "He gave me those first five years of security. He gave me Grandma and Colleen and Judy to help me through the worst years. And then, of course, He gave me you, my only stability through all those shaky times."

"Yeah, and He saved you from death more than once, and He gradually brought all your plans to nothingness, cut off all your exits but Him." We were really getting excited. Maybe I did have something to share.

"Jimmy, I've often wondered why God's Word didn't hit me so hard in the hospital, after my abortion that time."

"Honey, from what you've told me, you were still not ready then, still too much on an ego-trip. You know, 'God saved me because I'm so good, rather than because He's so good.' We'll probably never really know for sure, but He did turn all that bad into good. Look how much more you've got to say to people now."

And it was true. I could talk about drugs, depression, abortion, suicide, jail, materialism, lesbianism, a failing marriage, hard-heartedness, sexual desires. But was I willing to?

Over the next couple of months, as I spoke more and more often, that question gradually answered itself. I "graduated" from telling people I was an "entertainer" to a "dancer," but that's all the farther I could go.

"They love You, Lord, not me. They won't accept me if I tell all," I protested. I couldn't or didn't want to admit that it was I who couldn't accept myself. But the Lord wasn't going to let me go so easily. I don't know how many hundreds of times my Bible fell open to the passage, "Confess your faults one to another" (James 5:15 KJV). I felt He was telling me, "Judy, Barbara Streisand is an entertainer. You were a prostitute."

Finally I could stand the tension no longer. By holding back, by refusing to trust Him and His people, I wasn't giving God the freedom to work in my life. One day, two whole years after I had been converted, I finally blurted out the truth at a women's luncheon.

"I'm going to tell you ladies something I have never admitted to Christians before, and I'm scared. I can only pray that you have love in your hearts, because you're going to need it." I could barely go on, my voice was quavering so badly. What had I gotten into?

"I wasn't an entertainer. I was a prostitute. A hooker. A whore. And I'm sorry."

The room was perfectly still.

"Oh, God, I am so sorry," I sobbed. "Please forgive me. I know You have forgiven me. Please help these ladies to forgive me, too."

For about two minutes, that's all I could say, I was crying so hard. When I finally dried my eyes and looked up, I couldn't believe what I saw. The whole audience was in tears, and, as a body, they rose and gave me a standing ovation. I knew they weren't applauding my past life or my prostitution, but the Spirit of God in me Who had prompted me to call it up from the past, bring it out into the light of day, and thus end forever its power over me.

"Tell us more," they begged, and I proceeded to tell them how I loved the Lord to the bottom of my being. I had cried to Him out of the depths, and He had delivered me. I told them that they, too, could have Him in their lives if they invited Him in and exposed themselves to His Word and His people.

After I was finished, everyone wanted to speak to me, to reassure me that they loved me and accepted me, but one incident touched me as no other could. That day, out of the audience, came five well-dressed, respectable women, all independently of each other, all of whom had pasts similar to mine.

"I was a prostitute, too, and I've never told anyone until today," they all said. Each of these women received the Lord that day, and each has remained faithful to Him.

I was drained at the end of that meeting, but it was a good kind of tiredness, the kind that comes after having run a long race and knowing that it will go easier and smoother the next time. As I sat on the empty stage in the empty auditorium, I told God how I felt about what had happened.

"Of all the things I have ever done in my life, Lord, this has blessed me the most. Thank you for showing me what You want me to do." Never, in all my years of stripping, of being on TV, of fame and notoriety, had I received more satisfaction, more joy, for now I was working not for money, not for fame, but for Him. I was rich beyond telling. My peace was past understanding.

After that I found, as most Christians do, that the more I opened my heart to God, the more He came into it; the more I gave Him to work with, the more work He could do. However, even to this day, one incident from my past still haunts me: my "sins" against my two sons. Nothing I did in those years pains me like that does, and I would give almost anything to be able to start over with them, to hug them and kiss them as children and watch them grow and prosper from little boys on up.

As of today, Gary and I have a good relationship, but Chuck, who is in his late teens and still lives with MaRue and Ardean, understandably wants little to do with me. I am reaping what I sowed, and although I am convinced God has forgiven me for the hurt I caused them, I still find it hard to forgive myself. I still wake up more nights than I care to count, and wander through the quiet house, thinking of both of them, praying for all of us, and crying silent tears over all those misspent years. I love them both so much, and my mother's heart cries out to them to fully forgive me.

I also know that the Lord is good, that He showers blessings on us more richly than we deserve, and that He heard my prayers of loneliness for my sons, because in June of 1972 once again I heard the words, "Judy, you're pregnant."

"Jimmy, we're having a baby!" I remember yelling. Everybody thought we were crazy. We hugged and danced and cried and laughed and shook everyone's hand in the doctor's office.

That night, quiet in bed, we talked.

"Honey, I've never told you this, but I've always wanted a little girl," I said. "But before, I was afraid if I had one she would turn out like me."

"That's all over now, babe."

"I know. Oh Jimmy, I want a girl so much—to dress her in ruffles, curl her hair, put patent leather shoes on her tiny feet. Can we pray for a girl?"

"Tell the Lord you want a girl, that a girl is the desire of your heart," he said. "Then tell Him that most of all, you want His will to be done." We then prayed together, dedicating our unborn child to the Lord.

Seven months later, a baby was born. A little girl we named Malia. The nurses thought Jimmy was crazy when he sneaked in each night at two A.M. to visit me in my hospital room. He got off work at 1:30 and couldn't pass up a chance for one last visit. And, after we'd talked, he'd tiptoe down, down to the nursery, press his face against the glass and stare at his sleeping daughter, all seven pounds of her.

"You know, Jimmy, I think there's one person I'd really like to introduce Malia to," I said after I brought her home. "My mother."

"Mom," I said when I called her, "I've got a new granddaughter for you to meet." ("And a new daughter," I thought.)

I prayed a lot on the way home, first in the plane and

then on the train. What would it be like, seeing Mother again? How would I feel? I'd only been home one other time since I'd left fifteen years ago, and that was for Dad's funeral. Now I was coming home again. What would greet me as I got off that train?

She was different than I had remembered. Softer. More mellow. Older. As the train pulled to a stop, I looked closely at her face. What I saw there was so familiar to me, it gave me a pang. Suffering. She had suffered, too. In her own way. In ways I'd never been aware of when I was little and hurting so badly for myself.

"Mother!" I thought. I could hardly wait to get off the train and introduce her to Malia. I know now that that visit with her was truly a blessing from God, for finally I was able to see my mother through His eyes instead of my own. Where my human understanding failed, God was giving me His divine discernment. As we took long drives and lingered over lazy dinners, I caught little glimpses of what it must've been like for her in the days of my youth—loving my real father (the man whose picture I had found in her dresser) but never marrying him because her family disapproved of Mexicans. Married to a man whom she must've sensed was cheating on her, not only with other women but with her own daughter as well. Never having enough money. Being nervous and irritable and unable to get her life together.

"Oh, Mom," I wanted to say to her. "How sorry I am for the pain that was in your life. How sorry I am that I wasn't old enough to understand."

She, in turn, seemed to be treating me with more respect than before. We had talked about my conversion, and the evidence of it was surely written all over me. I like to think she saw Christ through me, and that it was He Who commanded her respect. I wanted so badly to love her to the Lord, to let His love wash away memories of those past years as surely as it had washed away our sins.

"Oh Lord," I prayed each night. "Do for my mother what You have done for me." How different from the death wishes I used to have for her, for us all. Now there was only new life in my heart.

"You've been through a lot," she said to me one day.

"Yes, and I'd go through it all again if that was the only way I could meet Jesus," I told her. And I meant it.

The day before I left I drove around that little Oklahoma town. It was so small. So much a part of me. When I'd first arrived there, I'd thought to myself, "This is where I came from?" Now, as my visit was coming to a close, it seemed so natural. Of course, I'd come from here. I looked at Mother. This woman, this past, were as much a part of me as the baby snuggled on my lap.

The Lord had accepted me, my past and all, just as I was. Finally, I was ready to accept myself—the other woman and that new woman in the Lord.

Judy teaching Bible School at *Amarillo Woman's Jail*, Tx.

Pierre Moust

WRITTEN IN THESE TEARS

Written in these tears
     That are falling from my eyes
Is all the sorrow through the years
     And all my regretful lies

All the lonely days and nights
     Behind these prison walls
When all I had to do was to see His light
     And heed His heavenly calls

No my friend, these are not tears of saddness
     Nor are they tears of woe
They are tears of gladness
     For Christ Jesus, I do now know

by Randy Kinnaman
with the Holy Spirit

Love in Christ
Randy

ThanK you Jesus
I'm Free at last.

Written by inmate at Iowa State Prison

Epilogue

Much has happened to Judy and Jimmy Mamou since their conversion six years ago. From the very beginning, they could not help but tell others of the miracle that occurred in their lives. From this developed a radio program in which Jimmy shared the Gospel and Judy interviewed people on the streets, listening to their problems, telling them of the Solution she'd found. The program was aired on station **KAIM** in Honolulu, twice a week for two years.

Feeling a special burden for the downtrodden, both Mamous began visiting the prisons, the skid row districts, the half-way houses in Hawaii and in California, loving those they saw, sharing Christ with prostitutes, pimps, drug addicts and convicts. They also spoke in hospitals, colleges, churches and Christian meetings—wherever they were led.

Meanwhile, they studied and grew, Judy in a year-long Campus Crusade for Christ Leadership Training, both of them in Bible studies and theological classes.

In 1975 they went to Korea with the World Evangelism

Foundation, and in 1977 Jimmy participated in a Ralph Bell crusade in the Solomon Islands. Their ministry was expanding—everywhere there were people to talk to, listen to, share Christ with.

In June of 1976, Jimmy was ordained into the ministry. Shortly afterward, the Mamous sold all their possessions and moved to Southern California. Once again, they dedicated their lives to the Lord, this time on a full-time basis. They now speak anywhere they are invited, whether to one person or to one thousand. They are on 24-hour call to anyone, anywhere who wants to talk about Christ Jesus.

As such, they have no regular income, but rely solely on the Lord as their Source. They live on the faith that He will provide for them.

Judy once said, "When Jesus Christ pays my rent, He can tell me what to do." Daily, He tells her.

Daily, they feed on His Word.

They have never gone hungry.

If you wish to contact Jimmy and Judy Mamou they can be reached at the following address:

Jim & Judy Mamou
P.O. Box 100
San Juan Capistrano,
CA. 92675

P.S.

To the body of believers in Hawaii—You accepted us, cared for us, loved us and started us out in our ministry. You are all special to us and Hawaii will always be in our hearts. Mahalo!

To Leora Heim—You took me under your wing and taught me God's Word for four years. You loved me, prayed for me and taught me the importance of studying and obeying God's Word. For this I will be forever grateful.

To Mother MaRue and Dad Ardean—Your tender, loving care for me as a baby shaped my life and gave me the strength to go on when all seemed impossible. My feelings for you both cannot be put into words as there are no words big enough. You gave my sons hope in a world where there was no hope. Thank you for loving us both.

To my sons Chuck and Gary—My prayer is that you will forgive me for the mistakes I have made, and maybe one day you can find it in your heart to understand and to love me. But if you never forgive me, I pray you will always love God.

To my mother—I LOVE YOU!

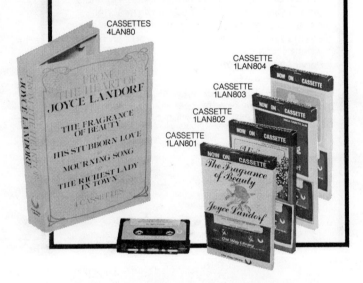